FIRST CLASS LEADERS

Fifty Principles
for Becoming a
Strong Leader

~

DR. BERNARD
GRANT

Unless otherwise indicated, all Scripture quotations are from the *New King James Version*, © 1979, 1980, 1982 by Thomas Nelson, Inc.

Scripture quotations marked (KJV) are from the authorized *King James Version*.

Scripture quotations marked (NIV) are from the Holy Bible, *New International Version*, © 1973, 1978, 1984 by International Bible Society.

Scripture quotations marked (TLB) are from *The Living Bible*, © 1971 by Tyndale House Publishers, Wheaton, Illinois.

FIRST CLASS LEADERS: Fifty Principles for Becoming a Strong Leader

Dr. Bernard Grant
Showers of Blessing Christian Center, Inc.
1740 North Raleigh Street
P.O. Box 2916
Rocky Mount, NC 27802
(252) 985-1848
fax: (252) 985-1360
email: tammyjackie@aol.com

ISBN: 0-924748-32-X
Printed in the United States of America
© 2004 by Dr. Bernard Grant

Milestones International Publishers
4410 University Drive, Suite 113
Huntsville, AL 35816
(256) 536-9402 x234
fax: (256) 536-4530
www.milestonesinternationalpublishers.com

Cover design by: Tony Laidig, www.thirstydirt.com

1 2 3 4 5 6 7 8 9 10 11 / 09 08 07 06 05 04

Contents

Contents

⊷ ≣◆≣ �

Foreword

I n every generation there are men of God who press in to a place in God to the degree that they stand head and shoulders above the rest. These are the men whom God uses to take that generation to the next level. Dr. Bernard Grant is one of those men. He is not only anointed to be a pastor and leader, but he also is anointed to be a pastor of pastors and leaders.

This book is a "must read" for every leader in the kingdom of God, both young and old. This book will help new ministers avoid many of the pitfalls that are common to ministry. It also will help seasoned leaders make the corrections necessary to take their ministry to that next level.

It is with great honor that I recommend *First Class Leaders: Fifty Principles for Becoming a Strong Leader.*

Dr. Robert L. Wilks, Jr., Pastor / Founder
Vine-Life Christian Fellowship
Riverside, California

Foreword

⊷ ⊰⊹⊱ ⊶

As in every area of life, we learn as we go. So it is when God has equipped and ordained one for the ministry. There are some lessons that you will never learn sitting in the seat at Bible school. Ministry, and more specifically pastoring, is one of the most challenging callings that one could have. Time of preparation is never wasted time. However, although years in the classroom can prepare us for teaching the Bible, they cannot give us the skills necessary to pastor God's people.

Dr. Grant has compiled principles that will cause the minister, who has the learning and the burning, to launch out into ministry and to bypass the pitfalls that those who have gone down that road have already experienced. More times than not, leaders start ministering without the proper equipment to succeed. The time is up for starting and not knowing what to do once you get out there.

This book should be a "must read" for anyone planning to enter the ministry. If a minister uses the 50 truths found in this book, he is assured that he has more to start with than the one who never had the privilege of gleaning from this prophet of God. Dr. Grant has a heart to see the minister win at all times, regardless of the challenges he faces. By taking this "head start" course that God has given to Dr. Grant, you will be off to the races and heading for success.

Dr. Torrance A. Jacko
Ambassadors Christian Center
San Diego, California

Introduction

When I began pastoring, I was a young man in my mid-twenties. I remember how I wanted to save the world. It was obvious that I was full of enthusiasm and zeal, yet I lacked wisdom in many areas. Although there were many ministry leaders back then, very few in my area had the instruction and training that I really needed. In His mercy, God allowed me to connect with a group of great men of God who would eventually become my mentors in ministry.

However, even with having some good men to follow, the most valuable lessons I learned came through trial and error. If I could have only foreseen each problem before it happened, I would probably be further ahead than I am now. Both you and I know that most people don't have the good fortune of knowing these things beforehand. I'm sure you have heard the statement, "If I only knew then what I know now…."

It appears that our lives would be far different if we had been able to avert some of the downfalls in life and in ministry. Nevertheless, the maturing soul recognizes that there is a certain dynamic that comes from "growing" through ministry-related challenges and learning lessons from those challenges that ultimately develop us into strong leaders. Some lessons we really need to learn and should not avoid since they help to shape us into what God desires for our lives.

So I went down to the potter's house, and I saw him working at the wheel. But the pot he was shaping from the clay was marred in his hands; so the potter formed it into another pot, shaping it as seemed best to him (Jeremiah 18:3-4 NIV).

Please understand that it is only after this shaping process that we come into the fullness of who we are. It is at that point that you realize God has given you a very genuine ministry, one that you should be proud to pursue. Once you accept that truth, you will not have to try to imitate your favorite world-renowned minister anymore. You will minister with a brand-new confidence, knowing that no one in this world can top you at being yourself.

As a young man going into the pastorate, I had a strong Christian foundation. I personally knew who Jesus was. I knew that He was Savior, Healer, Deliverer, and Lord of all. Those things I knew well. However, I did not totally understand His followers quite as well. Just like all humans are different in one way or another, all Christians are different also. It is those differences that cause ministers and leaders to make some striking discoveries about people.

One of those that I learned early on was that leading a congregation was really not about preaching great messages, having a Grammy-award-winning gospel choir, or having a huge congregation to brag about to fellow ministers at ministers' conferences. Simply put, pastoring is all about people. It's about knowing what makes people cry and what makes them laugh. It's about being there for those people collectively as a congregation when they need you the most.

It is all about leading the sheep that Jesus has entrusted to your care, into far greener pastures than they would have ever imagined without your guidance. It is your job to minister the

Word of the Lord with such power that people are transformed through the hearing of God's Word. What I learned was that ministering is all about the people and not about me. That was my first revelation.

My second revelation came as somewhat of a shock to me. Although it was relatively naïve of me, I came face-to-face with the reality that God's children were not always who they professed to be. They were not all nice and sweet. They didn't always keep their word. Some of the people who I invested time and resources into became jealous of my family's prosperity. And at times they told outright lies about me. When those things happened, instinctively I put up my guards. I became a bit cloistered as a means to shelter myself from pastoral abuse.

It became increasingly clear to me that everybody who came through the doors did not necessarily require my personal attention as they thought they did. In fact, very few needed that kind of attention. The majority of the people needed me to show them line by line in the Word of God *how* they could live a better lifestyle than they had ever dreamed of living before through applying biblical principles.

It would seem as if most people would be extremely excited about the opportunity to be taught truth that would make them free. But that was not always the initial response that people gave. Many people responded to my love and acts of kindness with great suspicion and mistrust. They'd been burnt by the world before and they didn't want it to happen to them again, especially by a minister.

Most people in our modern society carry great amounts of baggage wherever they go. From one state to another, from one country to the next, their luggage follows them. They carry their luggage from the past into their marriages and on new jobs; they use it as an excuse for why they cannot succeed in life; and they bring it with them to the altar when the invitation is offered to join the local church.

New York Times' best-selling author and leadership expert John C. Maxwell reminds us that "hurting people hurt people." God has entrusted His leaders with the awesome task of ministering to hurting people. It has always been my objective to minister God's uncompromising Word and His love to these hurting people. But how can we effectively do that without being hurt in the process? That is why I wrote this book.

As I already mentioned, there are some lessons you will have to learn on your own. However, there are far more lessons that you can learn through someone else's experience. In this book I have sort of volunteered to be your example of what to and what not to do in ministry. Yes, I'll admit I have made some mistakes. But it is not the mistakes that disappoint me. What disappoints me is when I don't learn from my mistakes.

It has been said that only a fool will make the same mistake over and over again. My goal is not to be a fool. I have always asked myself, "What positive thing can I learn from this experience?" The lessons that I learn far outweigh the failures. Perhaps that is why the enemy tries his best to get leaders to focus more on their failures than on the valuable lesson that they should learn from their failures. For it is that which will inevitably make you a strong leader.

First Class Leaders: Fifty Principles for Becoming a Strong Leader is a guide for Christian leaders to follow who need insight on handling problems that few ministers want to admit they've ever gone through. My heart's desire is to help every ministry head, every leader, every pastor with this message that God has given me, to be able to do the work of the ministry without unnecessary distractions.

For your convenience I have listed 50 of what I believe are the top issues that leaders either deal with on a daily basis or will eventually deal with in time. Each item is listed, commented on, and then concluded with the final authority on the matter: *the Word of God*. The thoughts and comments on each section are not very long, but they are timeless in their worth. If this book had only existed when I began in the ministry, navigating through the tough spots in my ministry would have been so much easier.

It is my prayer that you will use this work as a guide to steer you through the tough spots that you are in or one that you may be getting ready to go through. I believe that many leaders and ministers who read this book will learn how to avoid compromising areas altogether. Read it; pass it on to a fellow minister. Even your ministry people will benefit from this knowledge, for it will give them an insider's view on how a leader should be treated. Take the guesswork out of this great calling of God. You may not have every answer, but you have 50. I trust that each nugget is as valuable to you as it has been to me.

> *I charge you therefore before God and the Lord Jesus Christ, who will judge the living and the dead at His appearing and His kingdom: Preach the word! Be ready in season and out of season. Convince, rebuke, exhort, with all longsuffering and teaching (2 Timothy 4:1-2).*

About the Author

D r. Bernard Grant was born in the inner city of Brooklyn, New York. He received Jesus Christ as his personal Savior at the age of 15. He graduated with honors from A&T University in 1986. He received his Doctor of Ministry from Friends International Christian University in January 2000.

Dr. Grant ushers in the refreshing breeze of God's Spirit in a world divided, even fragmented by political, social, ethnic, and religious hostility. He seeks to keep unity as he pastors a non-denominational Church, where the Word is used to teach about faith, relationships, family, children, and finance.

Dr. Grant has a daily radio broadcast and a weekly television broadcast, as well as a broad tape ministry.

He is married to the former Gloria Phillips. They have two daughters, Rachel and Rebecca.

1. Never give positions to people simply to get them to stay.

I have known many ministry leaders and pastors who were guilty of giving their unqualified and oftentimes uncommitted members lofty titles and high offices in the organization or church as a means of getting those people to stay with their ministry. This is a horrible way to try to produce loyalty in a person. Yes, if you are just starting out in ministry, you need the support and strength that come with numbers. However, don't be afraid of losing people. Otherwise you will fall into the trap of doing whatever it takes to appease people instead of leading them.

Giving a person a position won't make him any more loyal to you than giving a fundamentalist Muslim a high rank in the Army will make him loyal to the United States. Titles don't produce loyalty; having the right heart does. The way that I promote people in our ministry is by watching individuals who don't even have a desire for a position. I watch them to see how effectively they perform without a title.

I want to know if that person shows up on time. I want to know if that person will stay longer hours than usual just to complete a task that needs to be finished. The attitude that the person has behind his service gives me pertinent clues as to whether or not he needs to be promoted. There have been people to whom I prematurely gave titles and positions and who still left my church.

It is better not to promote such people because, if they leave your ministry, it can cause the other members to wonder why someone in authority decided to leave. That's a formula for potential chaos and disorder in the house. Now, if you have done this before, don't get into condemnation over it. Just don't ever do it again!

The Bible presents a scriptural method for promoting people to offices in the local body that would serve all organizations well. Since every position of leadership is a position of service, the most universal scriptural application is that of the deacon. The word *deacon* comes from the Greek word *diakanos*, which literally means to serve. In its initial context this word was meant to depict a waiter or waitress serving tables. Therefore, the person who merits a high position or promotion needs to be the first and greatest at serving.

Jesus communicated quite plainly to His disciples that the road to greatness in the kingdom of God is through serving. He made it equally as clear that there are no other alternate avenues. Either you serve or you choose to exalt yourself. The latter road ultimately ends in destruction.

What are some earmarks of a person whose priority is service? Enthusiasm is a must. If you ask someone to serve in some capacity in your ministry and he shows low enthusiasm, then he has automatically disqualified himself from any future promotion. There also must be respect. Those whom you promote need to be reverent not only unto God but also unto man.

I have a friend who pastors a church. He shared with me how, when his church was only about two years old and had less then fifty members, he appointed a woman there to be over the children's ministry. This lady was exceptionally gifted to minister to children. She had plenty of credentials, having been trained at Willie George's ministry and Mark Harper's ministry—two of the finest children and youth ministry training centers in the world.

Even though this woman had great skills and the children absolutely loved her, she had zero respect for the pastor. At that time the pastor was about twenty-eight years old and this lady was in her late forties. The pastor was living a righteous life and possessed great vision. Nevertheless, she could not see herself submitting to someone whom she thought she was old enough to mother.

As a result, no matter what the pastor asked her to do, she never seemed to agree with him. She continued to remind him of her credentials, and she would say things like, "I've been doing this kind of ministry before you were born. I really don't need anyone's suggestions." Needless to say, her relationship with that ministry lasted about six months. For the pastor it was a miserable six months.

Never give anyone a position who does not honor the pastor or leader. Some people are quick to say, "I honor God, and Him only will I honor." When you hear someone start talking like that, it is a clear sign that he does not have the respect for leadership he needs to hold any position of authority. The truth of the matter is, if a person really loves and honors God, it will be evident in how he treats the leaders who God sets over him. Remember that!

Paul cautioned us not to give positions to double-tongued people. Double-tongued people are deceitful and untrustworthy. These people are often double-minded as well. You cannot give a promotion or position to a person who does not keep his word. When a person does not keep his word, he is clearly letting you know that he is unreliable. Unreliable people have often developed a tendency toward lying.

No one who has trouble with lying can hold a position of authority. Liars make hideous leaders. When Paul told Timothy that a good leader should be *"not given to much wine"* and *"not greedy for money,"* he was trying to convey the message that leaders and servants need to have discipline.

If a person is an alcoholic, he cannot serve in leadership. I am not suggesting that you kick an alcoholic out of the church. These people have a right to hear the Word of God like everyone else does. In time they will become disciples. But until then, don't promote them. It will only be an opportunity for the enemy to bring a reproach against your ministry.

So before you promote, check out a person's character. Be sure that he is filled with the Holy Ghost and exercises godly wisdom. Finally, make sure that the individual is a praying person. If a person doesn't possess these qualities and still insists on having a position, let him go and find another group that is willing to promote him. Your ministry is far too valuable.

Likewise deacons must be reverent, not double-tongued, not given to much wine, not greedy for money, holding the mystery of the faith with a pure conscience. But let these also first be tested; then let them serve as deacons, being found

*blameless. Likewise, their wives must be reverent, not slan-
derers, temperate, faithful in all things* (1 Timothy 3:8-11).

*Therefore, brethren, seek out from among you seven men of
good reputation, full of the Holy Spirit and wisdom, whom
we may appoint over this business; but we will give ourselves continually to prayer and to the ministry of the word*
(Acts 6:3-4).

First Class Leaders

2. | *Your lifestyle speaks far greater volumes than your words.*

———— ❦ ————

When I was fifteen years old, my mother up and moved our family from Brooklyn, New York, to a small country town in North Carolina called Bolton. Now, in Brooklyn, I attended the worst high school of the area. Drugs, cheap sex, and alcohol were readily available, and the gang lords and drug dealers "lived large" in our eyes. My mother, however, foresaw the future and without giving us any notice, announced we were moving to the South. It was a total culture shock.

When I arrived in Bolton, North Carolina, I thought that I would bring a taste of Brooklyn to these country folks. I would show them how we "got down" in Brooklyn. Unbeknownst to me, God had a totally opposite plan for my life.

My first summer there I met a girl I was interested in. She was a member of the Church of God in Christ, and she asked me to come to church with her on a choir rehearsal night. I didn't have anything else to do, so I went. The only reason I went was because I wanted to get with her, and I thought going with her to church would increase my chances at winning!

After the rehearsal she asked me if I would come to a Sunday morning service with her. The people at the church were pretty nice, the choir wasn't bad, and I didn't have anything on my schedule anyway, so I went. I had no idea what I was getting myself into. The presence of the Holy Spirit instantly captured me. I remember accepting Jesus as my Savior after the preacher asked if there was anyone who wanted to be saved.

After having been exposed to the dark side of reality, now I was exposed to a far greater reality—the light of Jesus Christ. Even though I was a new babe in Christ, I told God, "God, if You are not going to be better than drugs, sex, and the gangs, then I don't need You. But if You can be better than all that stuff, then I want You." From that moment on, God has been everything to me that He promised to be, and more. And more than anything else, I desired to live a lifestyle that was holy and acceptable unto God.

So as a teenager I accepted the truth that my life and the way that I live before humankind spoke volumes more than the words that came out of my mouth. Please don't misunderstand me; I believe in the power of words. I ascribe to the tenets of the word of faith. However, I am mature enough to realize that just because someone can talk a big game does not necessarily mean that he can back it up.

Realizing that God is and always has been a God of action, I knew that I too would have to follow His example by acting on my words. God doesn't just "say"; He actually does what He says. And He expects His sons and daughters to live the same way—with integrity in word and deed. As a result, it has always been my desire to not only be known as a man who wins people to the Lord, but also a man who lives a life that pleases God.

I do not believe in or condone the actions of any man or woman of God who lives any kind of way and expects everyone else to just accept it. Although all believers are held accountable to God for their actions and conduct, leaders are held to a much higher standard because of the authority and responsibility they hold. Knowing that forced me to discipline myself in areas where others have failed. The Bible gives many accounts of men who have failed because they succumbed to one of three main areas of temptation: Power, Money, and Sex, or PMS.

You need to resist every symptom of PMS that tries to overtake you. These three areas have killed and emasculated more great men and their ministries than I care to count. The way to overcome PMS is very simple, yet the repercussions are profound if you refuse it. Stay humble. Give money away. And men, stay away from women.

Let's face it. Ministry leaders and pastors have power. Whether you are leading ten people or ten thousand people, you sit in a seat of power. It doesn't really matter how others view you in that seat of authority as much as it matters how you view yourself. Humility is the only cure for leaders with big heads and prideful spirits. Remember what happened to Nebuchadnezzar? Maybe you are on top today, but there is no guarantee that you will be tomorrow. Your attitude will always project the most accurate outlook for your future. Stay in humility. If you can't handle power, then go do something else.

I actually have two suggestions for guarding yourself against the abuse of money. First, designate a group of sanctified believers to handle the counting and depositing of offerings and income. Although I believe the leader or pastor has the authority to make Spirit-led decisions regarding large money issues (such as building improvements, foreign missions giving, etc.), he still needs to have a group to help him in the decision-making process.

Now, I don't mean a group like the traditional deacon board that continually usurps authority over the pastor. No, I mean a group of helpers who can assist in making decisions that enhance the overall effectiveness of the ministry. Most importantly, these people who help with finances can defend the minister if he is ever falsely accused of mishandling funds.

My second suggestion is simple: Be a big giver. Every ministry organization and its leader should be ready to give at the Lord's command. Always be ready to empty out your account and sow seeds into other ministries. Giving cures avarice and greed. I've never met a greedy giver. That doesn't even sound right—that's like saying you met a fat skinny person. One cancels the other out. The more you give, the less chance you have of being enticed into fiscal self-indulgence.

Finally, leaders, don't make advances toward the opposite sex. Men, don't flirt with women, and please do not counsel them without prayer and protection. By "protection" I mean counseling women with your wife present if you are married and with another seasoned believer as a witness if you are not married.

Although that advice may sound a bit old-fashioned, following it can help you prevent a whole lot of heartache, pain, and shame. Your reputation before God is far greater than what some wanton woman thinks about you. Guard yourself and your spirit! This same counsel goes for women who are in ministry. Be careful to protect your interests and your good name. You may be totally innocent of charges that the enemy may bring against you. However, you should never put yourself in a position to let your good be spoken of as evil. Leaders, keep your flesh under the blood of Jesus.

If you've chosen to walk the walk and talk the talk, then I urge you to find some men and women to whom you hold yourself totally accountable. Remember, people who love you will speak the truth to you. They won't allow you to get puffed up in pride. They'll warn you when they see tendencies toward PMS. Please believe me, I am not condemning you if you have failed in any of these three areas. God will restore you if you have fallen.

The problem is that although God forgives, sometimes people will not. Neither do they forget. The impression that you have left on the heart of someone who believed in your words cannot be easily erased. So as you prepare to lead and stand before people, ask yourself one question. "Can I honestly say that I am living a lifestyle completely congruous to what I am about to say?"

If the answer is yes, go ahead and speak. If the answer is no or even maybe, or if you are totally unsure, correct those areas of your life quickly. If you will do so, the next time you stand before people and speak, your words will literally be drowned out by the more voluminous actions of your life. That's the message that people really need to hear.

For God did not call us to uncleanness, but in holiness (1 Thessalonians 4:7).

Now may the God of peace Himself sanctify you completely; and may your whole spirit, soul, and body be preserved blameless at the coming of our Lord Jesus Christ. He who calls you is faithful, who also will do it (1 Thessalonians 5:23-24).

3. | *Beware of anyone who is too eager to get close to you.*

I have always been a bit concerned about people who are eager to get close to me. Now, I am not saying that I am unsociable. I love people. However, I love the anointing of God on my life more and will go to extreme measures to protect that anointing.

When someone joins your ministry or church, the first thing he needs is to be discipled in the Word. She doesn't need to have a private session with you. He doesn't need to serve you by holding your bags, being an armor bearer to you, or taking care of any of your personal needs. When people try to muscle their way into my circle, I intentionally try to push them out. You see, I believe that God is a God of purpose. If God wants me to be close to someone, He will make it happen. It won't necessarily happen overnight, but it will happen in time.

If it is God's intended will for a person to become part of my circle, then *He* will create the atmosphere for healthy growth to occur. The ministry and outreaches that God has afforded me to build and oversee are great. They took many years of prayer, sacrifice, sowing, and then waiting for the harvest to come in.

It takes time to build greatness. However, greatness can be destroyed in a second. Be aware.

On September 11, 2001, two planes crashed into the Twin Towers, imperiling thousands of lives. Those towers took years to physically construct. And even before the actual building began, there were years in the planning and development stages. Yet, in less than one hour, both towers crumbled, burying lives in the ashes.

When I think about how quickly such marvelous structures were destroyed, it makes me very cautious about whom I allow to come into my life. When people are too eager to get into your company, yet have not invested any quality time in getting to know you first, you need to proceed with caution. No relationship is built in a moment. Strong relationships always take time to build if they are going to last.

If you are a leader with vision, you probably don't have too much time to waste anyhow. I know that I don't. With that in mind, you need to be very careful and selective about who wants to get close to you. Every person who says he wants to serve doesn't necessarily want to serve. Some want to serve only to get in close enough proximity to you to destroy you and your family.

My family and I are far more valuable than the Twin Towers in New York City. Unfortunately, our government was not discerning enough to prevent Islamic terrorists from getting too close to us. Because of that, far too many casualties occurred. I pray that you will never experience a casualty in your family or in your ministry. Let only those people into your inner circle whom you have taken the time to know, not just meet.

And we beseech you, brethren, to know them which labour among you, and are over you in the Lord, and admonish you; and to esteem them very highly in love for their work's sake. And be at peace among yourselves (1 Thessalonians 5:12-13 KJV).

4. | *Always keep your word.*

Before you say yes or no to something, get all the facts. If you will do this, you will decrease the likelihood of having to go back on your word. Actually, as a child of God, there should never be an excuse for you to not keep your word. When I was growing up, the old folks used to say, "Your word is your bond." That meant your word is like a binding agreement. It is like a covenant. Once it is set in motion, it should not be broken.

There are some leaders who don't run around with women. They don't steal money. They are not alcoholics. However, they do have trouble keeping their word. If you lack integrity regarding your word, I have news for you: Not keeping your word is just as sinful as sexual impropriety and drunkenness. If you commit to doing something, then just do it.

When I was a child, the five-and-dime store was booming all over America. (What we know today as Dollar Stores in many ways emerged out of the concept of five-and-dime stores.) Back then there were certain stores that would allow regular and loyal customers to sign a lined ledger journal signifying their commitment to pay for the goods that they charged on credit.

This was not a credit card. It was a notebook journal pad. There was no address or telephone number on the journal. The only information that was on the journal was the customer's name, the date of the purchase, the amount of the purchase, and exactly what items were purchased. They didn't even have the customer's social security number. If a customer said he would pay, then that was all that the proprietor needed to hear. The customer's word was enough.

Imagine if this same policy was in effect today. How strong would businesses grow employing this method of credit? It's pretty obvious that businesses would be forced into bankruptcy because of people's failure to pay. Ask yourself this question. "If the same type of service was extended to people like me, would these businesses stay alive or would they fail?" The answer to that question determines whether or not you are a man or woman of your word. Although we emphasize what we consider to be cardinal sins, it is equally as sinful and unrighteous to not keep your word.

Your worth is measured in the same way that God measures His worth: through keeping His Word. There have been leaders and pastors who have made promises to me that they have never kept. The sad thing is that they don't even care. So many have become so accustomed to not doing what they promised that for them it's normal behavior. You will never build anything of lasting value until your word becomes good.

God built an entire universe using His Words. He created the heavens and the earth with His Words. He made sea creatures and flying fowl using His Words. Out of nothing God called into being (with His Words) the sky and the oceans. Even when He made you and me, He did it with Words. We are made in God's Image, which means that we are like God. Since we are made in God's Image, He expects that we will take our word as seriously as He does.

In the Scriptures God never divides His Name from His Word. His Name and His Word are one. In fact, God declared that He would wage the heavens and the earth as collateral if He would ever break His Word. Leader, make it your highest priority to keep your word and your name inseparable. Make it your goal that when people think of you they can truthfully admit that you always keep your word.

In the same way but to a stronger degree, keeping our word is keeping our covenants. Many people do not understand or value the covenants that they make. A covenant is a commitment, and God blesses those who understand the value of keeping covenants. On the other hand, there are consequences for those who break covenants. This is an area that Christians across our society need much understanding about. Loyalty and commitment have become forgotten concepts.

We have seen how disloyal husbands are to their wives and vice versa. Millions of Americans have watched news reports of how major corporation heads defrauded their loyal stock investors. We have even seen Americans commit treason against our country by joining forces with our enemies. Even on a much more shallow level, long distance service providers will call and make you offers to try and get you to change from your existing service. They tell you that they'll pay you money if you will break covenant with your current service provider.

With so many examples of disloyalty and covenant-breaking around us, we must continually bathe ourselves in the Word of God, especially concerning this matter. God, who is our Chief

Example, was "married" to Israel. She was a bride who literally went whoring after other gods. She was unfaithful, yet God still remained faithful to her because of the strong value He placed on covenant.

As a pastor, I realize that the people whom I minister to do not belong to me but to the Lord. Nevertheless, I am still obligated to communicate the truth to them. And the truth is that you and I need to teach our people what it means to be loyal. Many people get angry over a message that they think you should not preach and will subsequently leave the ministry. Whatever happened to loyalty? Still others will shy away from the ministry after they hear a totally false rumor about the leader. Where is the covenant?

I used to think that people automatically understood covenant. That was one of my biggest mistakes. People will never understand the meaning of true covenant without human intervention. They must be taught. You have to tell people in plain words that you expect them to be loyal to you and the ministry. You need to teach your people that God honors them when they are faithful not only to their family, but also to their local church and their pastor.

Sometimes people have to choose between family members and serving God. If they have been properly taught about covenant, then the choice to follow God is not even an issue. Their decision is then birthed out of a heart of love for God rather than out of forceful manipulation. More people within your ministry would "cut covenant" with you if you only taught them the high value of this union. The basis of strength in any union starts with a commitment to covenant.

The grass withers, the flower fades, but the word of our God stands forever (Isaiah 40:8).

Then Jonathan and David made a covenant, because he loved him as his own soul (1 Samuel 18:3).

5. | *Beware of the person who has a problem with your prosperity.*

Y ou need to mark the person who has a problem with your prospering, particularly your prospering financially. That person can have a major destructive impact on your ministry if you allow him to. I have heard of people who did not want to bless their pastor with finances because they viewed him as their equal and thought that he should work a nine-to-five job just like everyone else to get the things people need in life.

If you have a person with this mind-set in your ministry—and such people always seem to be around—be careful that you do not allow that person close to you. Don't let that individual into your inner circle. Nothing exposes a person's true love for you more than when they express their heartfelt care for your prosperity. In fact, when someone invests into your life, he is proving his love by that investment.

When Jesus was at Simon's house, a woman came to pour very expensive oil on Jesus' head. It seemed that this was the least she could do to minister unto her Lord. When she poured out the oil, some people became very offended by this lavish display and began asking questions. Even one of Jesus' disciples inquired about the situation. The people wanted to know why this precious ointment was not put to better use. In their eyes, a better use of the oil would be to sell it and give the proceeds of that sale to the poor. This woman's choice to present an expensive offering caused her to be harshly criticized.

Things are no different today. People will criticize you for offering your best monetary gift to a man or woman of God. But wait a minute...if you decide to purchase a wide-screen plasma television set for Super Bowl Sunday for $7,999.00, do you think you will be criticized? More likely you will be commended. Yet, you will only use the television sporadically considering your weekly schedule. I have even seen fifty-two-inch screen television sets in the ghetto, in housing projects!

No one seems to think that spending that kind of money on a television set is wrong—even though you don't own a home. But if you give that same amount of money to a Christian leader or minister, some people can become a bit disgusted and claim that you should have done something more constructive with your money. Keep a careful eye on anyone who has that kind of spirit. Such individuals will never be a genuine help to your ministry.

Not only that, but eventually they will cause others to become disgruntled complainers just like they are. The end result will be detrimental to your ministry; it will become progressively unfruitful. You need people around you who love you enough to sow into your life so that you can fulfill God's purpose. Money is and always has been a tremendous acid test to determine who is with you, from who is not really dedicated to you.

The world says it this way: "Put your money where your mouth is." In short, if you say that you love someone, then your money will prove that what you are saying is so. Jesus put it another way. He taught that you will always know where a person's heart and dedication are by following where he invests his money. Make sure that the people who claim to be with you are backing up their words with financial substance.

> *And being in Bethany at the house of Simon the leper, as He sat at the table, a woman came having an alabaster flask of very costly oil of spikenard. Then she broke the flask and poured it on His head. But there were some who were indignant among themselves, and said, "Why was this fragrant oil wasted? For it might have been sold for more than three hundred denarii and given to the poor." And they criticized her sharply* (Mark 14:3-5).

> *For where your treasure is, there your heart will be also* (Matthew 6:21).

6. Never trust a non-tither; he is under a curse.

━━ ⊨◆⊨ ━━

The person who chooses not to tithe is under a curse and a closed heaven. Such a person cannot be trusted. I have no reservations in making that truth known. This is an area that more ministers need to be forthright about. If a person consciously robs God of the tithe, he is capable of doing anything sinful.

For the most part leaders and pastors who teach about the tithe do so because they need to meet their budgets. They believe that if they don't teach on it, their ministry's bills won't get paid. The rationale for teaching about the tithe should go far beyond temporal needs. The main reason you should teach about tithing is to break the curse off of the people within the body of Christ. The person who willfully chooses to ignore the Word of God concerning the tithe is a potentially dangerous person, and any association with such an individual can put you in harm's way as well. Why? According to Malachi 3, the curse associated with this sin was put on the land.

When a person robs God, the devourer is not rebuked, and his land becomes unfruitful. The implications of this blight are far-reaching. If the land is barren, the entire community suffers.

Everything within a civilized or uncivilized society revolves around the land and its ability to produce vegetation. If the heavens are closed and the skies are prohibited from sending down rain, then nothing will grow. Any attempt at tilling the soil and preparing the ground for a harvest will be useless, for nothing can ever grow out of parched soil.

If nothing can grow, then in time the people will die from starvation and lack of proper shelter. Everything in the land exists as a result of God's blessings. If the land is cursed, the people will inherit the fruit of the curse since they live there. In this same manner when a person does not tithe, he represents or becomes cursed soil. Nothing good can come out of him. And his only way to be redeemed from the curse is through repentance.

One famous preacher used to say, "I won't get in a car with a person who robs God. That person can't hold my bags or even give me advice." Many years ago this famous preacher was invited to preach at a church in Chicago. When he arrived at the airport one of the armor bearers came to pick up the traveling preacher in his freshly washed and waxed car. This young man blithely said, "Sir, I have been sent to pick you up, and I'll be your driver for the week. I am here to take care of all your needs."

The preacher asked the young man, "Are you a tither?" The young man dropped his head in shame and said, "No, sir, I have not been tithing faithfully, although I know that I should." After hearing that, the visiting minister immediately told the young man to pull the car over. He asked the man to call the church and ask them to assign him a new driver. He told the young man, "I've got a lovely wife at home. I've got four wonderful sons. I've got thirteen grandchildren. I want to live as long as I can to spend quality time with them. I'd be a fool to put my life in jeopardy by riding with someone who has no covenant with God."

Although that may seem to be a bit extreme, it really should not be. A person who understands the significance and Scriptural meaning of the tithe yet willfully chooses not to give the tithe to the Lord is at odds with the kingdom of God. His actions need to be taken seriously. According to the Scriptures, such a person is wicked, cursed, and in God's eyes likened to a thief who has jumped bail. When he is caught, he will be punished.

Someone may say, "I can't teach about tithing that strongly! It might make God seem like He is not a loving God, and I would not want to give that impression to anyone." Isn't it interesting that some folks believe that when you teach the truth, God may be misjudged or misunderstood; but if a person willfully chooses to disobey God's Word, he should not be held accountable for his actions. That's an unbalanced equation.

In plain words, don't allow anyone to be in any position of leadership or authority in your ministry who is not tithing. As I mentioned earlier, when people give you financial gifts it proves their loyalty and love for you. To a greater extent, though, when people faithfully give their tithe, it shows and proves their love toward God. It is impossible to love the Lord and not give anything to His house. Let's stop sugarcoating this topic and begin to use our finances to help further the message of Christ's kingdom.

Nearly all other religions of the world express an unfounded loyalty to what they believe. Consider even the terrorists who attacked our country on that unforgettable day, September

11, 2001. Those men were so dedicated to their cause that many of them gave more than eighty percent of their annual income to fund it. How much more should God's people, people who claim to love the Lord, fund His purposes? God deserves not only the tenth, but also our entire life. As leaders in the ministry we ought to collectively teach our people on the significance and sacredness of the tithe. It's a very serious issue, a kingdom issue. However, the people will never take it seriously until you do.

> *Will a man rob God? Yet you have robbed Me! But you say, "In what way have we robbed You?" In tithes and offerings. You are cursed with a curse, for you have robbed Me, even this whole nation* (Malachi 3:8-9).

7. | *Don't hang around visionless leaders.*

I n the kingdom of blind leaders, even a one-eyed leader is king. So it is important to keep company with those who are successful. If you hang around people who do not have vision, eventually it will impair your vision also. Once that happens, the people whom you lead will slowly begin to perish. For that reason, I don't keep company with small-minded people. I intentionally surround myself with people who are doing greater things than I am in their respective fields.

Of course, I would help anyone trying to get ahead and is serious about ministry. But I don't have time to waste with someone who is simply playing games, and neither should you. Leaders and pastors who complain all the time about the budgets they can't seem to meet, the buildings they can't build, and the members they can't attract, are not the kind of people I spend my time with.

Currently we have about a thousand members in our local church. I try to get around people who have two thousand, five thousand, and twenty thousand members. I ask them questions like, "What kind of strategies did you use to go from a thousand to two thousand? When I reach that level, what are some of the greatest challenges to overcome? How has your spiritual life changed since God elevated you to this level of responsibility and commitment? How long did it take to build your ten thousand-seat dome? What type of strategies do you use for hiring new employees? Have they always been favorable strategies? If you could do it all over again and start in ministry today with the knowledge that you have now, what are the top three things that you would do differently? What advice can you give to me as I continue to pursue the things of God?"

You cannot ask just anybody questions like these. The person who is qualified to answer those questions has earned the right. They are eagles. Please don't misunderstand what I am saying. I would never look down on or make fun of a person who has a small congregation and ministry. I believe that there is a place for everyone. I have friends who are pastors of small congregations, and I respect them for their commitment to serve the people whom God sends to them.

I love all my fellow brothers and sisters who are doing the work of the ministry. However, there are some people who are not going where I am going. They may love the Lord and be wholeheartedly committed to His cause; yet, they are not going in the same direction. Since I am a man of vision, I know without any doubt where I am going. The problem is that since I have never been there before, I am not always clear on how to get there.

When I surround myself with people who have already been where I am going, they help me to save time on my journey. They know exactly how to get there because they've been where I am going many times. I trust that God will allow me to be a mentor and visionary leader to not only my members, but also to up-and-coming ministers who desire to do great things for God. The people whom you keep company with will either enhance you or diminish you. Stick around people who know where they are going.

As iron sharpens iron, so a man sharpens the countenance of his friend (Proverbs 27:17).

8. *Avoid competition and comparisons.*

---◆--

Always judge yourself by yourself. Judge your ministry by your own ministry's standards. For example, if you are a pastor and your Sunday morning worship attendance averaged fifty people last year and this year you are averaging seventy-five people, then you have increased by fifty percent. The worst thing you could do is judge your ministry by what Dr. Fred Price or Dr. Creflo Dollar is doing. That is the formula for failure and chronic depression.

God expects you to increase at the pace that He has established for you. Just think about it for a moment. Pastor, if you have seventy-five or even one hundred fifty members and God decided to send five thousand new converts to join your church next Sunday, would you be able to handle it? Would you have the necessary structure in place to receive the people? Do you have enough ushers to serve five thousand people? What about your facility—does it have enough space? Do you have enough toilets? How many chairs do you have? Do you even have the amount of time required to train and develop these people?

The questions could go on and on. The point that I am making is that you probably would not be able to handle such growth if God gave it to you. There are some large ministries that pay a monthly mortgage of $200,000. That's a huge difference from the monthly lease of $2,700 that you are paying now.

Be grateful for what God has blessed you with. Utilize it to the best of your ability. If you are faithful over a few things, God promises to increase you. But if you continue to judge your ministry by that of another person's, or your messages by those of another, or your size by Dr. David Yonggi Cho's 750,000-member congregation, you've missed the whole point of ministry.

I have heard pastors try to justify their call to ministry by wearing alligator shoes or custom-made suits. So many young leaders get themselves into unnecessary debt by trying to dress and look like their favorite television evangelist. Maybe your favorite television preacher can afford to wear expensive clothing—and on the other hand, maybe he can't. Maybe he is putting on a front just like you are.

Personally, I believe that it grieves the Holy Spirit when we continue to compare and compete. I have heard leaders say, "Doc, how many members you got? I got two thousand. You should have seen how the people responded when I preached. Have you ever gotten a response like that before? How much money did you raise last week? We raised about $50,000." Who cares? God doesn't.

The real truth is that leaders who continue to compare and compete do so because they have an image problem. They are grossly insecure in their own gifting, talents, and abilities. When you know who you are in God, you never have to compete or compare anything. As you mature in the things of God, you'll begin to recognize that true success is not measured in stuff, membership, or how many tapes or books you've sold.

True success is measured by your willingness to do exactly what God tells you to do. If you do that, you are successful in His eyes. And that should be all that matters to you.

> *Oh, don't worry; I wouldn't dare say that I am as wonder-ful as these other men who tell you how important they are! But they are only comparing themselves with each other, and measuring themselves by themselves. What foolishness!* (2 Corinthians 10:12 NLT)

9. | *Let God get rid of your waste.*

＋─✠─＋

A healthy body will always have intakes and eliminations. If too much waste stays inside the colon, you'll inevitably develop colon cancer. In the same way, a ministry that contains wolves and goats too long will become spiritually cancerous. And just as cancer can spread like wildfire in the physical body, so it can spread rapidly in an organization or church. The best way to deal with cancer is to get rid of it fast.

One thing I have noticed over the years is that I have not had to ask very many people in my pastorate to leave. God has always done the job for me. For that I am very grateful. Obviously, if there is a person in my congregation who is attempting to destroy the sheep, it is my chief responsibility to protect the sheep and drive the wolf away.

If someone is trying to promote a heretical doctrine in our ministry, as the shepherd under the Great Shepherd, I cannot let such heresies go unchecked. So if a person continues to spread such teaching after he has been warned not to, I will have to ask that person to leave. Or if a spirit of Jezebel, the spirit of rebellion, or the spirit of ungodly lust shows up at my church and expects to plant itself there, I have to escort that spirit out the door immediately.

In other words, sometimes you have to be strong enough to ask someone to leave who has proven by example and action that he is trying to hinder the growth and spiritual development of your ministry. It's your God-given responsibility and assignment. In most cases, however, you won't have to do that. Usually people reveal themselves. People cannot hide who they really are but for so long.

The real person has to emerge in time. Whether a person is evil or good, in time he will be known and identified by the fruits that he bears. If the foundation of your ministry has beens built correctly, the devil will recognize that. He will know that your ministry is not a place where he will be able to set up shop easily. Added to that, he knows exactly what ministries he can go to and divide and conquer the sheep easily. He knows which ones have not been founded on God's Word.

If your ministry fits the latter category, don't bother reading any further than this section. Put this book down. Instead, pick up your Bible and begin studying God's Word. Start asking Him to destroy your old weakened foundation and create another one. If the foundation is weak, your members are very likely to follow the same pattern. Pray and seek God for answers concerning your ministry and whether or not you are functioning in the right ministry calling.

However, if your ministry has been built on the solid foundation of the Word of God, then you need not worry much about anyone trying to overthrow and undo what God has planted. From time to time God will simply flush out the waste material from your ministry. When God does this, don't go running after the waste trying to redeem it. Consider it a favor from the Lord that God has decided to release a major block-age that has been holding your ministry back. God has released them; now you follow in His footsteps and release them also. Your ministry will be healthier than ever before.

> *If anyone does not abide in Me, he is cast out as a branch and is withered; and they gather them and throw them into the fire, and they are burned* (John 15:6).

10. Expect nothing less than total loyalty from your inner circle.

I have noticed over the years that the people who are the most loyal to the ministry are usually the ones who have stuck with the ministry through thick and thin. The people about whom I've always been concerned are the people who are very gifted yet not dependable. Often people who are very gifted at preaching, singing, playing instruments, teaching the Word, or handling budgets can at times believe that their giftedness will compensate for their lack of faithfulness.

They begin to believe that they are indispensable. Satan convinces them that your organization cannot function if they are not there giving of their services. Unfortunately, in many cases Satan convinces leaders of this same lie. What you should never forget is that God's work will go on regardless of who does not want to properly align him or herself with your ministry. I have heard of pastors hiring musicians to play for their services who really do not have a heart for the ministry.

To these musicians, playing their instruments is simply another gig. It is no different than performing at a nightclub or at a casino. People who think this way will never help your ministry to become strong. I always expect total loyalty from the leaders in my congregation. Anything less than that would be unfair to them. The church should be the most respected and powerful institution in the universe. The reason why it fails to reach that mark of high distinction is because leaders and pastors fail to demand the type of loyalty that Jesus claimed would make solid disciples.

We have been guilty of spoon-feeding people for far too long. After a while people have to grow up. They must mature. A great part of that maturing process is when they understand the meaning of loyalty. In the corporate world, particularly in the publishing industry, large publishers will often ask their employees to sign an agreement vowing their loyalty to the company. In the event that they leave their job or if they are terminated for lack of service, they cannot seek employment with a competing company for a number of years after leaving.

Why am I mentioning this? Should we too ask our members to sign contracts vowing loyalty to our ministries? I do not believe that we should have to have anyone sign a contract. A person's word alone should signify his commitment. Unfortunately, I have seen over and again how people will join a church, and then the pastor will never see them again. That is a sad but true commentary on how our society has declined in their allegiance to their own words over the years.

Most church members and even people within your community have certain expectations of you as a leader and pastor. Above all they expect you to keep your word. I have no problem with their demands in this area. However, I too have expectations of them. I expect everybody in my congregation to keep his word. If you say that you are going to be committed, then I expect total commitment, not excuses. I would much rather a person be totally honest with me and let me know up front that he is just not going to be faithful. Then I would not have to waste time investing anything of value into that person.

Following Jesus is the most serious commitment that we will ever make in life. It is even more serious than pledging in a fraternity or a sorority. Although marriage is a sacred and God-ordained institution, your commitment to Christ far outweighs a commitment to even your spouse. Jesus' disciples left everything to follow Him. If it was good enough for them, it should be even better for us today.

> *Then Peter said, "See, we have left all and followed You." So He said to them, "Assuredly, I say to you, there is no one who has left house or parents or brothers or wife or children, for the sake of the kingdom of God, who shall not receive many times more in this present time, and in the age to come eternal life"* (Luke 18:28-30).

> *If anyone comes to Me and does not hate his father and mother, wife and children, brothers and sisters, yes, and his own life also, he cannot be My disciple. And whoever does not bear his cross and come after Me cannot be My disciple* (Luke 14:26-27).

First Class Leaders

11. | *Always hire the best you can afford.*

I f you want to have a quality ministry, hire people who excel in their fields and pay them as best you can. There is nothing worse than settling for "second best" in God's work. God's work should epitomize the best that this world has to offer. If there is any area where we should invest, it is in the area of ministry.

At the same time, don't hire people just to keep up with the ministry down the street. Sensible pastors always seek to maximize their ministry with limited resources. Just having people on staff does not make your ministry great. Having people on staff who have a heart for the ministry and who fill a needed position make your ministry effective.

Don't employ hirelings because hirelings are not loyal to anybody's ministry. They basically go from one paycheck to the next best paycheck. They do the work of the ministry for the sole purpose of money. You can't grow healthily with a person like that. Hire a person who knows that a paycheck is simply a by-product of his labor. Still, if you know that a person has a heart for ministry and he is qualified to lead in praise and worship, or as a musician, you should pay that person as well as you can.

I'm sure that you have heard the statement before, "You get what you pay for." That statement is true in every area of life. In the early days of your ministry you may not be able to afford the very best of everything. However, as God continues to prosper your ministry, share that prosperity. Even when it comes to building beautification, hire professionals who will help the building reflect the Image of God, not one of struggle.

If you make it a practice now to always utilize the best around you, after a while it will become a habit. Once it has become a habit, it will be a natural part of you and characteristic of your ministry to do things in an excellent way. People will begin to expect excellence from you all the time. The Bible teaches that the one who works deserves to be compensated for his work. Pay people well, for that practice will put your ministry at a level of excellence that money can't buy.

You shall not muzzle an ox while it treads out the grain (Deuteronomy 25:4).

12. | *Never use ministering times to bad-mouth others.*

O ne of the greatest time wasters is when ministry leaders and pastors use precious preaching and teaching time to demote other ministers and their ministries. An equally big time waster is when leaders and pastors use the same time to discount members who did something to make them mad. Leader, the time that God gives you to articulate His Word should be used very wisely. Time devoted to ministering should never be taken lightly. Every time you get behind a microphone, your whole goal should be to feed the sheep and build up the Body of Christ.

It doesn't matter how overlooked or abandoned you feel; it doesn't matter if someone has treated you badly—time spent complaining about it will never help your situation. You could fuss and complain until you are literally blue in the face, and nothing will change.

The average pastor in America has between 45 and 90 minutes each Sunday to give his congregation a life-changing Word intended to last them for at least one week. In some circles the preacher may take up to two or three hours to accomplish this same goal. Either way, sowing anything other than God's Word during that time is a complete waste of yours, as well as your hearers' time. It also shows that you have very little regard for God's time.

I have always considered it a privilege to be able to teach and instruct people in the ways of the Lord. Since time is my most valued commodity, I am very careful not to waste it idly, particularly when it comes to ministering the Word of the Lord.

I know a pastor in Dallas, Texas, who has been pastoring for more than twenty years. In its heyday his church had an active membership of about a thousand people or more. This brother is a first-class soul winner. He has an anointing to be able to get people to follow Jesus. That's his strength. His weakness is that he has always been overly critical of other people's ministries. He is always finding fault with other pastors and trying to find areas of their lives that do not meet God's standard, in his estimation.

Several years ago when Bishop T.D. Jakes moved from Smithers, West Virginia, to Dallas, Texas, to launch The Potter's House, several pastors in the area began to feel greatly intimidated. This same pastor was one of them. He began to regularly talk to his members about how they should not go to Bishop Jakes' church because he was all about showmanship and not about the spiritual matters.

After a while, this pastor's church had almost emptied out completely. The people became so curious as to whether or not their pastor's accusations were true that they began visiting The Potter's House. When they went there, they experienced the power of God in a way that they had never felt before. After so many visits they became hooked. This pastor lost nearly nine hundred members because the precious time that he was given to minister and strengthen the people, he used to condemn a fellow brother in Christ.

What he didn't realize was that he was actually advertising another man's ministry free of charge. He gave his members reasons to be curious about T.D. Jakes' ministry. If this pastor had a quality ministry, it really would not have mattered whether Bishop Jakes' church was in the next town or directly across the street from his.

The more you value the time you are given to minister, the greater your chances are of growing. When you choose to use that time for anything other than teaching God's Word, you are going to lose every time. In the case of this Dallas-based pastor, he lost big time. That kind of loss is just not worth it. Stay focused on the purpose that God gives you to teach.

> *Let no corrupt word proceed out of your mouth, but what is good for necessary edification, that it may impart grace to the hearers. And do not grieve the Holy Spirit of God, by whom you were sealed for the day of redemption. Let all bitterness, wrath, anger, clamor, and evil speaking be put away from you, with all malice. And be kind to one another, tenderhearted, forgiving one another, even as God in Christ forgave you* (Ephesians 4:29-32).

13. | Lead your family first in the Ways of God.

———— ⧓ ————

Y ou may win an entire city to the Lord. You may even win an entire nation to Jesus. But if you fail to win your family to the Lord, then you have failed miserably. If you want to lead a healthy and thriving ministry, make sure that your family life is in its proper place first. It will be very difficult for you to minister to someone else's children who need to get delivered from a crack addiction, if your child hasn't kicked the habit in years.

Make it a practice to instruct your family first in the Ways of the Lord. There are ministers and pastors who lead ministries and congregations, yet their marriages are in a mess and their relationships with their children are less than desirable. The first order should be to get your family back from the devil's clutches. You may ask, "Brother Grant, are you suggesting that I give up the ministry altogether?" That is not what I am saying. What I am trying to get you to understand is that reaching your spouse and your children are just as important as reaching the people in your city, state, or country for Jesus.

After all, your family is with you all the time. If there is anyone who you should be able to influence, it should be your immediate family. People will tend to evaluate your ability to lead them by judging how effectively you are able to lead your own family. This is only fair. It does not make practical sense for a minister to lead someone else's family where his or her family has not already been. Get your priorities in order. God is always first, and your family comes directly after. After you have led them, then you are free and equipped to win the universe.

For I have known him, in order that he may command his children and his household after him, that they keep the way of the LORD, to do righteousness and justice, that the LORD may bring to Abraham what He has spoken to him (Genesis 18:19).

14. | Pray in the Spirit at least one hour every day.

Prayer is the breath of life for a believer. If you do not pray, you will eventually die from a suffocated spirit. Leaders should pray with an even greater intensity knowing that they are responsible for the souls of many. Because of that, the enemy is twice more likely to plan an attack against leadership. The success that I enjoy is perhaps more connected to this discipline of prayer than anything else. Everything that I have had faith for, I prayed in the Holy Ghost, and God made each thing come to pass.

Even the structure that we built was birthed in prayer. The finances that were needed to complete the structure were not merely a result of having clean credit; prayer produced our provision. I follow this pattern in every area of my life. Whatever I am in need of, I pray it into the earth realm. I get up each morning and pray in the Spirit for at least one hour.

What am I doing, when I do this? I am building up myself in the Holy Ghost. I am praying the mysteries of God. There are things that I do not know how to pray for, yet when I pray in tongues (which is praying in the Holy Ghost), God gives me answers to questions that I have not even asked yet.

He who speaks in a tongue edifies himself, but he who prophesies edifies the church. I wish you all spoke with tongues, but even more that you prophesied; for he who prophesies is greater than he who speaks with tongues, unless indeed he interprets, that the church may receive edification (1 Corinthians 14:4-5).

For if I pray in a tongue, my spirit prays, but my understanding is unfruitful. What is the conclusion then? I will pray with the spirit, and I will also pray with the understanding. I will sing with the spirit, and I will also sing with the understanding (1 Corinthians 14:14-15).

But you, beloved, building yourselves up on your most holy faith, praying in the Holy Spirit (Jude 20).

Then He came to the disciples and found them sleeping, and said to Peter, "What! Could you not watch with Me one hour? Watch and pray, lest you enter into temptation. The spirit indeed is willing, but the flesh is weak" (Matthew 26: 40-41).

15. | Be confident of God's work in your ministry—and say so.

If you worked at McDonald's, it would not make a thimble full of sense for you to brag about how great Wendy's and Hardees' hamburgers are. In the same way, you need to boast about what God is doing in your ministry more than anyone else's. Some leaders simply don't use good judgment. They'll use prime time to advertise how God is using some well-known minister across town or in Chicago or Dallas. Yet they will never admit that God might perhaps use *them* to do mighty things.

I wouldn't want to be part of a ministry where the leader is not confident about God's wondrous working power in his or her own life. If God is moving in a church across town more than He is moving in my church, then maybe I need to move across town to that church. Your people need to be grounded in the fact that they are receiving the best ministry at your church. If you are not convinced of that, then maybe you don't need to be a pastor.

God singularly anoints men and women to lead people in unique ways. Bishop T.D. Jakes is anointed to shepherd the shattered. Dr. Frederick K.C. Price is anointed to break the spirit of poverty off of people and teach them how to walk by faith and not by sight. Pastor Benny Hinn is anointed to usher people into holy worship and break the stronghold of sickness and disease off of their lives. Joyce Meyer is anointed to teach God's people that there is hope after the enemy has tried to kill you emotionally and mentally.

Each minister has a unique gift and ability to articulate the truth of God's Word. One is not greater than the other. In God's eyes they are all great only when they are doing what they've been called to do. If you are teaching and ministering God's Word in the fashion that He has called you to teach and minister, then your service is pleasing unto the Lord. Beyond that, you should know that God also has called you to be you. And there is no one on this earth who can outdo you when you're being yourself.

If you don't like your way of ministering, why should anyone else? At Showers of Blessing Christian Center, I try my best to make it clear that there is no other ministry in our town and region as unique as ours. I am not suggesting that God cannot or does not move at other churches in North Carolina; I believe He does. However, I don't know that for sure because I don't attend every church in my state.

I do faithfully attend Showers of Blessing. And I can verify that the Word of God is being taught here regularly. There are hundreds of people who testify of how their lives have been changed since they've joined this church. There are hundreds of people who have experienced total life prosperity since they've become members at Showers of Blessing. These are cold, hard, proven facts that I know.

I can only recommend churches that I know are proven to minister to the people's needs. For example, if you lived in the Los Angeles, California area, I would recommend that you attend Crenshaw Christian Center where Dr. Frederick K.C. Price is the pastor. I am familiar with that ministry. Dr. Price and I have a relationship. I know his life and I know that he is a man of integrity and lives what he preaches.

But if you are in Rocky Mount, then I am convinced that the best possible choice for you is Showers of Blessing Christian Center. When you become convinced that your church is the most significant church in your area, the people who follow you will begin to believe the same thing. And when they begin to believe it, they will begin to share with their families and friends exactly what God is doing at your ministry.

They'll become eyewitnesses working on behalf of your ministry. When that happens, God will cause such a chain reaction to occur in your ministry that you won't have any-where to put the people who will flock to your church to be shepherded by you. But it all begins when you start to articulate to the people that there are tremendous benefits to becoming a part of your local church.

You therefore, my son, be strong in the grace that is in Christ Jesus. And the things that you have heard from me among many witnesses, commit these to faithful men who will be able to teach others also (2 Timothy 2:1-2).

16. Know where you belong and grow there.

❖ ❖❖❖ ❖

There are many streams within the Body of Christ. They range from Baptist, Pentecostal, and Word of Faith to Oneness Pentecostal, Methodist, Lutheran, Congregationalist, and so on. You can't grow everywhere unless you are a weed—and weeds do not serve a real purpose except to be cut down and thrown into the fire. You have to know where you belong and blossom there. Although I believe in unity within the Body of Christ, I also believe that you have to be grounded in what you believe in order to be of any benefit to anyone.

You can't just believe everything from everybody. Everybody is not right. On the other hand, everybody is not wrong either. It is only when you know where you stand that you'll be able to make sound judgments. We need each other in the body of Christ since each person brings a fresh dynamic to the whole. However, your people need what you have. And what you have should be a direct connection to what you have been feeding from.

If you have been feeding from everybody's pastures, you will more than likely become sick. It is true that God wants us to be one and joined together. Nevertheless, God does not want us to be confused. God never authored a book called Confusion; therefore, you shouldn't study that lesson. The quickest way for you to become confused is to open your spirit to everything and every teaching that is coming down the pike.

It may very well be that a new teaching has been beneficial to people in various ministries in your region. That does not mean that the same teaching will benefit your people in the same manner. Know what your assignment is. Master the art of being you. You have been given a specific assignment by God to impart what He has given to you to His people. Once you've accomplished that, you will be successful.

But that success will only happen when you have recognized, accepted, and become satisfied where God has planted you in His Body. Growth will only happen when you are connected to the right stream for you. There are certain trees that need a particular type of soil in order to live. If you uproot that tree and place it in a different kind of soil, it may not live. That does not mean that the soil is bad soil; it could very well be extremely fertile soil. The point is that the soil is not conducive for the kind of tree that is trying to grow there. So if you are not growing at the rate that you believe God has gifted you to grow, then maybe you need to check your soil. Look where you are planted and ask God if it is the right place for you. If it is, you will prosper in due season. If it is not, you will surely die.

There are diversities of gifts, but the same Spirit. There are differences of ministries, but the same Lord. And there are diversities of activities, but it is the same God who works all in all. But the manifestation of the Spirit is given to each one for the profit of all (1 Corinthians 12:4-7).

He shall be like a tree planted by the rivers of water, that brings forth its fruit in its season, whose leaf also shall not wither; and whatever he does shall prosper (Psalm 1:3).

17. Don't be afraid to admit that you missed it.

You will save yourself so much grief if you will just learn to be honest. Hopefully not all the time, yet every now and then you may say or even do something that is not in line with God's Word. When that happens, confess it quickly and move on. I am not talking about gross sins here. Perhaps you thought you heard from God on a certain matter, but it really was your zeal and enthusiasm that you thought was God's voice. And when you spoke, "Thus saith the Lord," it never came to fruition.

Just face it, you are human, and humans are subject to human failure. There have been leaders in situations like the one I just described, and instead of admitting that they missed it, they doggedly held on to what they believed, even though the Holy Spirit told them that they were wrong! Leader, you are not God. Only God is incapable of failure. To believe otherwise is nothing more than ungodly pride. And need I remind you that God hates and severely punishes pride?

About five years ago, a woman pastor received a call from a relative of one of her parishioners. This person asked the pastor to help her get back money that was owed to her by the pastor's church member. This caller told the pastor that she lent a certain amount of money in good faith expecting to receive her money back. The pastor felt a bit embarrassed by the situation. She didn't want the word to get out that she led parishioners who chose not to pay their debts.

On the following Sunday morning during worship, this woman pastor abruptly got up claiming that she heard a word from the Lord. She prophesied to the woman who did not pay her cousin back as promised, saying, "The Spirit of the Lord has spoken to me telling me that you will not pay your cousin her money. And God says that it's just not right. Repent, saith the Lord, and repay your debts, and God will forgive you."

At first this unassuming parishioner believed that her pastor was really hearing from God. So she possessed a reverential fear about the whole matter. That afternoon her cousin called her to let her know that she had called the pastor to give a report of her actions. Instantly this faithful member realized that the pastor had lied, claiming to have heard from the Lord concerning this matter, yet was operating in the flesh. It would have been far easier for the pastor to simply confront this lady in a mature, adult-like fashion. But because she did not know how to operate that way, she chose to use spooky and mystical tactics to convince her member to "heed God's Word."

When the parishioner confronted her pastor about the situation, her pastor denied everything. She told her church member that she really did hear from God and that her cousin did not tell her all the details. Feeling betrayed, this woman chose to leave the ministry.

What went wrong? First of all, this pastor should not have lied about anything. That alone is unacceptable. However, she made matters worse when she decided to try to conceal the matter. She should have simply confessed, "I'm sorry, sister. I honestly did not know how I to handle the matter. And because of that I acted in the flesh. Please forgive me." If the pastor had responded in that manner, this woman would have stayed with the ministry and her respect for her pastor would have been restored.

People are thankful and much appreciative when their leaders are plain and real. I have heard people of the world complain about this or that minister who appears to be so phony and fake. "They are so plastic," they'll criticize. Like the rest of us humans, you too have made mistakes that God has helped you to overcome. Letting people know when you miss God and get caught in predicaments helps them. If you can be real, then they can be real as well.

Leader, if you miss it, just confess it and let God dismiss it.

Pride goes before destruction, and a haughty spirit before a fall. Better to be of a humble spirit with the lowly, than to divide the spoil with the proud (Proverbs 16:18-19).

A proud and haughty man—"Scoffer" is his name; he acts with arrogant pride (Proverbs 21:24).

First Class Leaders

18. | *Exercise self-control.*

⊢ ⊷⊣≣⊢ ⊣

Before you can ask your people to walk in a discipline, they need to see an example of it—and that example should be you. Remember, people who are called to ministry are called to a higher standard of living, particularly since leaders represent the *Zoe* or God-kind of life.

For example (although I realize that this is not every minister's reality), all ministers should have great credit. All ministers should have their spending under control.

There are so many leaders and ministers who have horrible credit that it has really become a shame. Many Christians today—both leaders and laypeople—have their home phone numbers unlisted not for the sake of minimizing ministry-related calls to their home, but rather to avoid debt collectors. If your credit cards are up to the limit, then you need to cut them up, close each account, and pay the cards off. You don't need a prophet to prophesy a word from the Lord concerning this matter. You just need to exercise some self-control.

Perhaps your buddies are going to purchase some custom clothing. If you have not met your financial obligations and paid your monthly expenses, then custom clothing is just not for you. You will have to take a rain check. If you are in the season of becoming debt-free, then you can't go out with your friends every time they choose to eat out. It's not your season. There is nothing for you to feel bad about; it's just not the right timing.

God is far more concerned about you having integrity in an area of discipline before you go ask others to discipline themselves. Of course this applies to more than consumer credit spending. For example, God also wants you to exercise discipline in the area of your weight. You should not feel spiritually satisfied if you are grossly overweight. The Bible condemns the sin of gluttony in the same verse that it condemns sexual promiscuity.

If you preach against sexual sins yet weigh more than four hundred pounds, you too are guilty of the same sin that you are preaching about. Adultery, fornication, prodigal living, unrestrained spending, and gluttony can all be lumped under one category: lack of self-control. Indulgence in any of these areas proves one thing: that you need to exercise self-control.

I know that this can be a touchy subject for you, particularly when you have become satisfied with your habit. Nevertheless, my word to you is that you must break your out-of-control habit before it breaks you. Perhaps you need to fast more often to discipline your flesh. Maybe you need to spend more time in prayer. Whatever it takes, just make sure that you begin to control yourself. Your ability to do so will measure your capacity to lead God's people.

He that hath no rule over his own spirit is like a city that is broken down, and without walls (Proverbs 25:28 KJV).

Principle Eighteen

But I discipline my body and bring it into subjection, lest, when I have preached to others, I myself should become disqualified (1 Corinthians 9:27).

19. | *Confront issues promptly.*

D on't wait to deal with issues that arise in your ministry and among your people. Deal with sin quickly. It will save you enormous amounts of stress. Sin is like a cancer that, if left unchecked, will corrode the entire body in a short amount of time. You also should quickly deal with issues that have potential to become sinful. Though it may not be sinful in its beginning stages, if it is left alone it may cause tremendous amounts of damage to your ministry and possibly your reputation.

Eli, who functioned as the high priest, allowed his sons to commit sinful acts with the women who assembled at the doors of the tabernacle. These women were not just any kind of women. These women preserved themselves for the work of the ministry. They were devout and holy women of God who were virgins and intended to remain that way so they could wholly give themselves to the Lord. Eli's sons were full of perversion and did not respect the commitment that these women made to God.

They used fiendish tactics to persuade the women to have sex with them. I am sure that in some ways they used manipulative control over these women to force them to have sex, which is a type of rape. Even though Eli knew well what his sons were doing, and although he knew that their actions were socially illegal and warranted criminal charges and possibly death, he said nothing about it. And more than breaking the civil and criminal laws, these men were both in direct violation of God's Holy laws.

What I want you to understand is this. Had the father, Eli, reprimanded his sons through direct confrontation, God would have not destroyed them. God is and always will be a merciful God. Destruction is always the very last option. Destruction only comes to a person who has repeatedly failed to heed the warnings of the Lord. When we as leaders confront people about their indiscretions, our confrontations may literally save their lives.

It is obvious from reading 1 Samuel 2, that Eli's sons never had any home training. They were spoiled brats, typical preacher's kids who were never reproved. Because their father throughout the course of their lives did not properly discipline them, they lacked understanding on how their behavior would offend the Almighty God. It would seem that Eli's children would have been taught at the very least the do's and don'ts concerning God's Law.

After all, their father was a high priest. Unfortunately, he was not capable of successfully passing down his faith to his posterity. Whether these young men were related to him or not is also unimportant. As the high priest he should have known that discipline was needed in this situation. Because he chose to ignore the situation, his sons died. This lesson goes to show you that overlooking a situation never solves the problem. It makes it larger. Make it a habit to promptly confront matters so God won't have to.

> *Now Eli was very old; and he heard everything his sons did to all Israel, and how they lay with the women who assembled at the door of the tabernacle of meeting. So he said to them, "Why do you do such things? For I hear of your evil dealings from all the people. No, my sons! For it is not a good report that I hear. You make the LORD's people transgress. If one man sins against another, God will judge him. But if a man sins against the LORD, who will intercede for him?" Nevertheless they did not heed the voice of their father, because the LORD desired to kill them* (1 Samuel 2:22-25).

20. Pursue excellence in all areas of life and ministry.

The patterns that you set for your ministry when you get started will carry throughout as you grow. Therefore you must establish excellent procedures for your ministry early on. Start setting the precedence of excellence in everything you do, especially as you move toward the direction that you believe God is taking you. The fact that you are small and just starting out does not mean that you shouldn't do things in an excellent way.

Pursue greatness. You will never get big if you always think small. Little children always amaze me. When I listen to children who are three, four, and five years old, they are always saying stuff like, "I am a big boy. Don't call me little. Babies are little. I'm a man." It's these statements that set the pattern for development and growth in the little boy. Those statements usher them into manhood. They literally speak manhood into existence. It may take ten to fifteen years or so, but since they continually hear themselves saying those things, they receive the fruit of what they have heard for so long. Leaders need to follow this childlike example of faith.

In your ministry's formative years, you need to make a habit of doing things first class. For example, you should always—and I will reiterate always—start a meeting on time. There should be no exceptions to that rule. Regardless of how many people are present, whether there are ten, twenty, or even one hundred people, you should start right on time. I've been to places that have not made starting on time a priority. Now in their fiftieth year of ministry, they still start every meeting late.

Don't wait for a certain amount of people to show up before starting. Maybe you have never thought about it, but that is outright disrespectful of other people's time. I mean, if ten people showed up on time, why should they wait until the other ten arrive? Why should the ones who came on time have to stay in service twice as long, enduring the punishment for tardiness that their fellow brethren should have received? They really should not.

One of two things will happen if you continue to do this. The first possibility is that you will develop slothful spirits in the people whom you lead. You will never grow achievers by starting late. Most achievers have arrived at that point of accomplishment in life because they have spent their entire lives being on time. They show up for work every day on time. Every meeting that they are scheduled to attend they are on time.

So when they come to your ministry services, why should they have to experience lateness? Kingdom work should not be second-rate to the standards of the world. It is the Body of Christ that should set the standard of excellence in everything. That brings me to my second point. If you continue to do this, you will wind up losing all the achievers. Then you'll only have the limited capacity to minister to losers.

Losers hate to be on time and always make stupid excuses about why they continuously show up late. That is why most losers are impoverished, never experiencing the joy of life. As I have stated, even if you have ten people there, start on time. Achievers will be attracted to your commitment to do things like the big boys. Believe me when I tell you that they notice every little detail. And it is those details that will cause them to continue to attend your ministry and sow their tithes and offering there.

Another point of interest has to do with how you treat a guest ministry. When you have a small group and your budget is pretty constrained, you have to make wise choices about who you bring in. For example, all too often pastors of small churches try to make a big impression on their community and other local churches in town by hosting guest ministries that they simply cannot afford. That is not trying to do things excellently. That is a foolish blunder.

If you have an annual budget of $75,000, then you do not need to try to invite megaministries to your annual conference unless you have already established a covenantal relationship with them. Ministries that require millions of dollars to run often need large amounts of money to operate. If your ministry is not at that level, then you should not put yourself in a predicament that may only bring embarrassment to you and lack to your treasury.

Preaching and teaching the Word of God is what will make your ministry grow, not hosting famous ministers. In the beginning stages of your ministry you need to focus on building the people from the inside out. In order to do that you will have to invest time in teaching and instructing the people on what God's Word says and on what you expect from them. Anyone who you choose to invite should come with the mind-set and mission of strengthening the foundation that you have already laid. They should not be interested in promoting their own agenda. If that is the case, you might as well leave them where they are.

There are literally hundreds of thousands of qualified, godly, and anointed ministers who not only will appreciate the opportunity to minister at your services, but who also will do a wonderful job. Get accustomed to treating every invited guest with the same level of excellence as you would treat a well-known preacher.

In my book, there is no such thing as a celebrity or big-shot man or woman of God. The only big shot is the Lord Jesus Christ. All of God's ministers should be honored for their labor, yes. Do for them what you would do for others and you will be establishing a precedent that will carry over as God brings growth to your ministry. Give them the best offerings that you can possibly give. Put your guest in the absolute best accommodations that you can afford. Feed them at the finest restaurants that your budget can afford.

When guests visit your services for the first time, always send a letter thanking them for choosing your ministry to fellowship. If you can send them a special gift like a pen or a key chain with the ministry's name and logo imprinted on it, visitors will remember you after their initial visit. Make sure that you always have smiling greeters at the door to welcome everyone into the sanctuary at each service.

You really don't have to break the bank to do things in a first-class manner. The bottom line is that God expects you to run your ministry in an orderly fashion. Order and excellence are not traits associated with only large ministries. They are both intentional choices, standards you should set from the very first time you have your first service.

Let all things be done decently and in order (1 Corinthians 14:40).

21. | *Protect the anointing.*

O ne of the saddest Scriptures in the entire Bible is the passage that details the Holy Spirit's departure from Samson. Interestingly, when the Holy Spirit came on him, He did so with a grand appearance much like when He came on the believers in Jerusalem at Pentecost. But when the Holy Spirit departed from Samson, He did it so quietly that no one knew—not even Samson.

Delilah lulled Samson to sleep while she seduced him on her knees. When he was asleep, she called for a man to shave off all his hair. As a result, Samson became devoid of his strength. Although this narrative deals with Samson's fatal attraction to a woman, the meaning of this story goes far beyond the typical tale of a seductress who causes her victim to succumb to her craftiness.

No, this story really concerns God's anointing upon a person's life. The whole idea behind this story is that once you know for sure that God's anointing is on your life, you must do everything in your power to protect that anointing. The anointing comes, and when it goes it is gone.

It is not always a woman or a man who attempts to destroy God's influence on your life. It may not be a sexual thing at all. In fact, if you think that sexual temptation is the only enticement seeking to draw you away from God, then the devil has you exactly where he wants you. The enemy will continue to deceive you when you put all of your focus on one area, particularly the wrong area. There are many areas in which the enemy may come to try and destroy you. The most obvious one to the believer, while the most overlooked by the carnal, is the area of pride.

Pride is the original sin. It is the very sin that cost Lucifer his anointing—the anointing that enabled him to praise and worship God in heaven. Because of pride he was literally thrown out of heaven. His pride was so strong that he never apologized for his insolent behavior. In fact, he began concocting ways in his corrupt mind to try to overthrow the kingdom of heaven. His pride made him believe that he could actually pull it off.

For you have said in your heart: "I will ascend into heaven, I will exalt my throne above the stars of God; I will also sit on the mount of the congregation on the farthest sides of the north; I will ascend above the heights of the clouds, I will be like the Most High" (Isaiah 14:13-14).

If a spirit of pride catches you out, you must surrender that evil spirit to Jesus at once. Pride, more than any other thing, including sexual immorality, will cause a person to lose the anointing on their life permanently. Samson's problem was not merely a lust problem. His problem was one of pride.

Samson believed that he could not be taken down. He began to believe in his heart that his strength was unmatched and that God would always empower him to get the job done. What he failed to realize is the same thing that so many ministers today fail to recognize: Although God can use you, He is not dependent on you. God can get the job done by simply raising up another generation to do what He asks.

This is a trap that I have seen many well-known ministers fall into. Their pride somehow causes them to believe that because they minister to thousands of people, write books, have worldwide television broadcasts, and air on radio every day that they will always have God's presence and provision on their life. They are absolutely wrong.

No matter how high you think you have traveled up the ladder of spiritual success, you will always be required of God to demonstrate a spirit of humility. Humility will keep you at the top. Pride will tumble you to the bottom. Once you begin to believe that you are the one who is responsible for your success, you are only seconds away from losing your anointing. Protect the anointing of God on your life. Flee sexual immorality, but just as importantly flee pride. The spirit of pride will always guarantee a great fall. Beware!

> *Then she lulled him to sleep on her knees, and called for a man and had him shave off the seven locks of his head. Then she began to torment him, and his strength left him. And she said, "The Philistines are upon you, Samson!" So he awoke from his sleep, and said, "I will go out as before, at other times, and shake myself free!" But he did not know that the LORD had departed from him (Judges 16:19-20).*

22. Look to the children for clues as to what their parents really think about you.

— ❧ ⸭ ❧ —

N ormally if a man's children turn cold toward you, that man has too. One thing that I know for sure about children is that they cannot hold in what they are feeling. Most of the time children will blurt out the things they have heard said in the home. It's so unfortunate that children are uprooted from the loving environment of a local church when their parents become disgruntled about frivolous things. It seems so unfair that after their children have become accustomed to the surroundings where they are growing in the Spirit and are beginning to bear fruit that they are so abruptly taken away.

When children in your ministry, who are normally friendly and bubbly, begin to act a bit funny toward you, that is a telltale sign that those parents have been speaking ill against you. I have always preferred knowing up front if someone is not with me than to find out way down the road when it may cause far more damage to the ministry and my family. So note what the children do.

Children are inherently honest creatures. They inherit that nature from God their Father. If they hear negative things about you, they are going to believe those things, whether they are true or not. On top of that, children automatically believe anything their parents speak. Always remember that children are by nature very loving. They won't transform from a loving creature to a monster unless they've been programmed to.

So you will always be able to use children to measure and gauge exactly where their parents stand. In fact, some parents are such cowards that they actually use their children to communicate their complaints and feelings on their behalf. If you want to know what's really going on, ask the child. A little child shall lead you.

Indeed everyone who quotes proverbs will use this proverb against you: "Like mother, like daughter!" (Ezekiel 16:44)

23. | *Don't keep company with people who are sexually immoral.*

Y ou become the company that you keep. If you know that someone is a sexually immoral person, a drunkard, or an idolater, then you who claim to know Jesus should not hang out with that person. If you continue the relationship, eventually you too will begin to take on the same sinful traits that that person practices. By keeping company with them you are condoning his wanton behavior. It's an altogether different situation if it is a brother or sister in the Lord who is in sin and chooses to repent of that sin.

In such a case you are obligated to forgive that brother or sister and help him or her to be restored. The Bible says, *"Brethren, if a man is overtaken in any trespass, you who are spiritual restore such a one in a spirit of gentleness, considering yourself lest you also be tempted"* (Galatians 6:1). But if someone is continuing in habitual, unrepentant sin, you should distance yourself from him.

If you choose not to distance yourself from the person, then both the people within the body of Christ and those who are of the world will begin to view you in a negative light, believing that you share in the same actions. If you have made up your mind to be a person of godly convictions, there are some relationships that you have to boycott. Everybody who is in your company today is not necessarily going to go where you are going in life.

Instead, keep company with those who are pure in heart. The only reason you should spend time with immoral people is for winning them to the Lord and a lifestyle of holiness. If believers are practicing immorality, it could very well be that they have a reprobate spirit. That is a spirit that you do not want to rub off on you. So be careful and select your company wisely.

> *I wrote to you in my epistle not to keep company with sexually immoral people. Yet I certainly did not mean with the sexually immoral people of this world, or with the covetous, or extortioners, or idolaters, since then you would need to go out of the world. But now I have written to you not to keep company with anyone named a brother, who is sexually immoral, or covetous, or an idolater, or a reviler, or a drunkard, or an extortioner—not even to eat with such a person* (1 Corinthians 5:9-11).

24. | *Remind yourself that you are not called to reach the whole world.*

There are different kinds of ministries for different kinds of people. It always amuses me when I hear leaders say, "My ministry is called to reach everybody." When I hear that, I know that the minister more than likely leads an ineffective group. A statement like that may sound really powerful and evangelical, but in actuality it's just not true. God has not called you to reach everybody.

Even Jesus, the Head of the church, did not reach everybody. That is why He called you and I. We are to reach those whom He could not. The apostle Paul was sent specifically to reach the Gentile people. Gentile people were his complete focus. Peter was called to the Jews. So Peter never deliberately proselytized unbelieving Gentiles, for they were not his target market. Both of them knew whom they were called to reach, and that's why they were successful.

You can't mix water with oil. Neither can you mix different vision statements. Whatever God has given you as the vision for your ministry is tailored just for you. It's when you are confused about whom God specifically called you to reach that you begin to try and make your ministry relevant to everybody. It is at this same point that your ministry fails to reach anyone.

If you run a ministry whose primary goal is to raise up leaders, you probably should not target a group of people who have no desire to be leaders. That will only frustrate your results. Perhaps it is your calling to minister to the affluent in society, realizing that they too need to hear the message of the Gospel of Christ' kingdom. If that were the case, it would be ridiculous for you to establish your ministry in the heart of the ghetto where you can be guaranteed that the affluent will not travel to.

On the other hand, if God has called you to minister specifically to poverty-minded people, it would not make any sense for you to start your ministry at the Ritz Carlton grand ballroom. Poverty-minded people would feel uncomfortable in palatial surroundings. They won't show up because they will feel as if they don't belong.

You have to know who your target market is. If you can't ride or even support the weight of a Harley Davidson motorcycle, why on earth would you start a ministry to bikers? That's not using sound judgment. If you were called to minister to the illiterate, it would probably create an unbalanced equation if you were a Rhodes scholar. If you are going to be effective, you have to know the type of people that God has called you to reach.

There are some ministries whose primary aim is to raise money for foreign and domestic missions. That's the reason why those ministries exist. Every message is somehow based on the harvest and our Christian responsibility to go out into that harvest and reap souls. For them prosperity is interpreted in terms of giving money to the foreign field. A person who leads this type of ministry may frown on another leader who drives a Mercedes Benz car, believing that the money spent on that car could have been sown in the missions field.

What he does not realize is that the leader who is driving the Mercedes Benz is probably called to another calling in the kingdom of God. He's probably called to develop millionaires who in turn can sow millions of dollars to every good work. Looking at it from that point of view, each of our distinct functions becomes a whole lot clearer. And it should become clearer to you that each ministry has a specific reason for being.

So let each one give as he purposes in his heart, not grudgingly or of necessity; for God loves a cheerful giver. And God is able to make all grace abound toward you, that you, always having all sufficiency in all things, may have an abundance for every good work (2 Corinthians 9:7-8).

When a leader begins a ministry, the ministry should have a specific reason for existing. Why do we need another ministry when there are so many out there? What makes yours any different from the ministry across town? Suppose you are starting a church in the same town as the church that you left. Is your church clearly different than the one you previously attended? If not you need to go back to that church and help strengthen its cause since yours is absolutely the same.

Our ministry sows money into other ministries that are doing what we are not skilled to do. We've sown money into Dr. I.V. Hilliard's drug rehabilitation ministry at Light Christian Center in Houston, Texas, because we believe in what they are doing and are convinced that Jesus died to redeem all sinners.

However, we do not have the twenty-four hour facility at this point and time needed to help people who have made a commitment to breaking this binding habit.

So that brings me to this conclusion: I can only effectively help those whom I am equipped to minister to. If I am ill-equipped, then I will come up short every time. It was natural for Peter to reach Jews since he was a practicing Jew himself. Brother Nicky Cruz, author of the best-selling book *Run Baby Run*, can successfully lead thousands of drug dealers and gang bangers to the Lord since he too was delivered from such a lifestyle. God allowed Moses, a Hebrew, to be raised in pharaoh's Egyptian quarters as his formal training to one day become a deliverer to his people. In the same way God will use you in a very singular way to produce extraordinary results for Him.

Here's a list of questions that I would like you to answer. As you answer each question it will help you identify exactly who God has called you to reach and why.

1. Why has God called you to lead a ministry? Obviously He wants you to reach people who cannot be reached by any other person in the world, but even more specifically, why *you*?

2. Begin to ask yourself the question, "What kind of people am I called to reach?"

3. Who do I naturally attract?

4. What is my training and background?

5. How can I use my training and life experiences to help people?

As you answer these questions, the Holy Spirit will reveal to you who you are called to. Knowing who your target is will make your life so much easier since God will take out all the guesswork, allowing you to focus on the one or perhaps two things that He created you to do. You cannot do everything, yet God can. Find out what your part is and do that.

As for those who seemed to be important—whatever they were makes no difference to me; God does not judge by external appearance—those men added nothing to my message. On the contrary, they saw that I had been entrusted with the task of preaching the gospel to the Gentiles, just as Peter had been to the Jews. For God, who was at work in the ministry of Peter as an apostle to the Jews, was also at work in my ministry as an apostle to the Gentiles (Galatians 2:6-8 NIV).

25. | *Never be afraid to talk boldly about money.*

<hr />

D r. Ralph Wilkerson, pastor emeritus of Melodyland Christian Center in Los Angeles, California, always says, "Whatever you want to see in your church, preach and teach on it and you will have it." That advice is very true. I have had ministers ask me, "Doc, how do you get your people to give money and sow sacrificially?" The answer is simple. I teach them. What you teach is what you get. The problem is that most ministers are literally scared stiff to talk about money. And that is the only reason they don't have it.

If you are a part of that fearful group, then you will never have money and your ministry will never meet its annual budget. Again, most leaders are afraid of what their people might say if they get on that forbidden subject. "Oh, there he goes again talking about money. Can't we ever hear a message that doesn't have to do with money?" You choose not to teach on the topic since you are afraid that visitors will not come back because they were offended when you preached on "How to have whole life prosperity."

No matter what people think or how much they complain, you cannot compromise when it comes to teaching about giving.

Everything that your ministry needs to do to impact the world for God will take money, and plenty of it. You may say, "Brother Grant, we need more prayer in our ministries. That's what we need to teach more on." I agree wholeheartedly with you. But prayer always produces major results.

After God answers our prayers, souls are going to be saved by the thousands. When those souls are saved, they are going to need a place to learn how to be a disciple. So you are going to need to house these people in a rented or owned building. That is going to cost money. You may need to construct a building or maybe rent a hotel ballroom for at least a year or two. In addition to that, you are going to need books and manuals to teach from, and they are not free. It costs money to publish books and print them. The ongoing expenses relative to ministry are usually high, if your ministry is making a real impact in the world.

If your building is paid off and you are not really touching lives within your community, then you really don't have a great need for money. In that case, don't bother teaching on it. But if you are like me, a person who is hungry for souls to be saved, then you have got a lot of ministry on your spirit waiting to be birthed. You've got buildings to purchase. There are whole neighborhoods that have been overtaken by drugs and violence that you are determined to claim back for God. In order to do that, you are going to have to purchase each property one by one, and that is going to take money.

How about that senior citizens' housing complex? The Bible commands us to take care of our widows and seniors. It is our responsibility to make sure that the elderly have stellar accommodations suitable to their needs. We need life centers for our families and our youth. We must build safe centers where teenagers can come and get a physical workout and at the same time hear about the love of Jesus.

I believe that the Body of Christ ought to help our graduating high school seniors go to college. Collectively the Body should come together and sponsor scholarships that will pay full college tuition for aspiring young men and women. Our children and youth ministries have ongoing needs for new props, curriculum, up-to-date games, field trips, DVDs and videos, and state-of-the-art audio and video equipment. Yes, we even need our own banks.

The people in our ministry need to be able to come to our own institutions and borrow, invest, and save their money. We need to stop being so dependent on the world's banking system that will readily take our money but will put us through the wringer when we need to borrow money to erect buildings or even buy homes. Each and every one of the things that I mentioned cost plenty of money. In this era it is virtually impossible to conduct effective ministry without money.

Whatever you can do without money, I will prove to you that you can do a thousand times more with money. Genuine men and women of God are not afraid to talk about money. In fact, that is one of the ways that men and women of God are measured. If you are truly sold on souls, you won't be the least bit afraid or intimidated to communicate to the people the financial need connected to reaching those souls. If someone has something derogatory to say, it really won't matter at all. If someone falsely accuses you, it won't make much of a difference when your heart has been fixed.

People always try to put Jesus in this false category as someone who was dirt poor and never really talked much about money. The real truth is that Jesus talked about giving more than any other topic. The parable of the sower is a parable that describes the process of possession in the kingdom of God. It simply states, "If you sow a seed, expect to reap a harvest." The message is really that simple, yet million of people all over the world still miss it.

Jesus warned us that if we did not understand this parable, it would not make any sense to learn any others. Understanding of all the Scriptures is predicated on this concept of sowing and reaping. The much quoted John 3:16 validates the truth of what I am saying. God so loved the world that He sowed a seed named Jesus and reaped a harvest called you and me.

If people leave your ministry because you talk about giving, they weren't going to give anyway. If they get mad about your giving, it is only because they are broke and stingy. So if they get mad or leave, you've really lost nothing. You weren't going to get anything from them in the first place. Those who stay and hear the Word and receive it with gladness will be prime candidates to receive the overflow of God's very best.

If you desire God's best for your ministry and the people involved in it, then do them the favor of teaching on biblical stewardship. You may be falsely accused. So what? Jesus was falsely accused too. You know that you are not teaching for the sake of greed and avarice. The money that you receive has a specific mission involved, and that is to reach those who are lost and to help sustain the God-ordained leaders of that effort. That should help you to stay focused and totally ignore anything that the critics will ever say about you.

Therefore, whether it was I or they, so we preach and so you believed (1 Corinthians 15:11).

So then faith comes by hearing, and hearing by the word of God (Romans 10:17).

For where your treasure is, there your heart will be also (Matthew 6:21).

26. | *Always trust what you are sensing in your spirit.*

＋◦ ≣◆≣ ◦＋

Quit judging whether you are hearing from God or not. Usually when your spirit is speaking, it's God speaking to you. The reason I know this is because most of the things that you sense in the spirit are not things that the devil would tell you to do. For example, the devil is not going to tell you to put $10,000 in the offering.

He is not going to tell you to raise up a ministry to win lost souls. You sensed in your heart that God wanted you to be a financial blessing to a widow, yet you questioned whether it was really the voice of God. That shouldn't have been a difficult thing to determine. The devil is out to destroy widows and orphans, so he wouldn't tell you to help them!

If you are a child of God, His Spirit will lead you. Not only that, but you also will sense the peace of God about whatever you are doing. My advice is that if you don't sense the peace of God concerning any decision you are contemplating, then don't do it. When your decision is God-based, you will have His peace to go along with it. Sometimes when you are acting in faith, you will feel somewhat sensitive. That's not a bad thing.

Anytime you are doing something by faith, you will always have a feeling within that says, "If God doesn't do this, it is not going to happen." That feeling is good. It's normal. But even when you have that feeling, you should still sense God's peace within your spirit. One thing that I have discovered over the years is that when you don't follow your first response to the Holy Spirit, you will inevitably miss it, time after time.

There have been times when I had to beat up on myself after not following my first spiritual inclination. Every time I question whether or not I should do it, give it, or say it, I always regret not listening to the first voice that I hear. And it is usually God's voice that you will hear first, particularly in important matters.

When you hear His voice, humbly respond with a confident, "Yes, Lord." If you begin to make a practice of responding affirmatively to the still small voice, after a while you will begin mastering the art of hearing and obeying God. The rule of thumb is, if you sense the peace of God, it's because it *is* God!

And let the peace of God rule in your hearts, to which also you were called in one body; and be thankful (Colossians 3:15).

27. | *Don't marry methods.*

———— ⊰◆⊱ ————

A lways be willing to change. What's working for you this
year may not work next year. The way that you did ministry in the 1960s is probably irrelevant to the times
that we live in today. Of course, Jesus Christ is the same in
terms of His nature. He will always be Healer, Savior, Deliverer,
and Sanctifier in the Holy Ghost. Those things will never
change about Jesus Christ.

However, the ways that His Spirit moves and the ways that
He manifests on His people have been changing for thousands
of years. Why? Because God will never become predictable. As
soon as you can predict what you believe God is going to do,
He'll change on you just like that. God refuses to be put into
a box.

There are some things that are just not working in your
ministry that may need to change. There are some pastors in
my city who have pastored for more than thirty years. They
pastor twenty or thirty people, yet they continue to hold services several nights in the week. I would think it is pretty obvious that they are putting a drain on these same poor people

service after service. But their reply is, "I've been doing this for thirty years, and I am just not going to change for nobody."

The person who thinks like that will never get favorable results. They always have what they always had because of their refusal to change. Maybe if they changed from having so many services to just two each week the attendance might increase. The problem is that they'll never know if that would ever happen because they refuse to change.

You may need to change the times that your service begins and ends to make it more accommodating for the people you are called to serve. It doesn't matter what the conventional times are; you have to follow the prompting of the Holy Spirit for yourself. You cannot get too comfortable with how things used to be if you are going to be on the cutting edge. If it is no longer working for you, then change. Try something different. In fact, keep changing until you discover what is right for you.

I know a pastor who leads a really strong church. After countless difficulties with his church choir, he made the decision to not have a choir at all. Initially the members thought that the pastor lost his mind. In their city, having a church choir had become such a normal practice that to do otherwise would make people question whether or not you were really a bona fide church. That didn't make any difference to this pastor. His conviction was that if there was continual fighting and confusion in the choir, then the choir did not need to meet.

He said, "God is not the author of confusion. And this choir is bringing nothing but confusion to all of us." So his choice to close down the choir was also a choice to end the confusion that had lasted, in his opinion, for far too long. Amazingly, after closing down the choir, his congregation grew to more than a thousand faithful parishioners. People began to come to church for the Word. No one seemed to care if the choir ever came back. The Word was so relevant and life-changing that they continued to come and grow because they were receiving a proper and balanced spiritual diet.

The choir was not formed again until seven years later. That may seem like a long time to you. It might also seem a bit radical. But in this man's ministry, phenomenal results were produced. Just imagine what kind of results you might possibly get if you were to make a drastic change in your ministry. Your results might just be miraculous. Now, don't change just because I suggested the change. Change because God has prompted you to do so. I promise you that if God ordered the change, He will also provide the growth that accompanies the change.

> *For as many as are led by the Spirit of God, these are sons of God* (Romans 8:14).

28.

Always know the men and women you allow to minister to your people.

Y ou are completely responsible for who you allow to minister to your sheep. If a guest speaker preaches total heresy, it's your fault. Therefore, it is never out of order for you to simply ask a guest minister, "What are you planning on preaching today?" If the person cannot tell you, you may not want him to preach. I have made it a habit of asking guest ministers to preach in my church who minister under a special anointing with a particular topic.

There are some ministers who are especially gifted in the area of prophecy. Others are gifted in the area of healing. Some ministers are explicitly directed by God to deal with finances and debt-freedom in the life of believers. Wherever the anointing is greatest in a guest minister's life, I need to know that. It's when I am totally clueless as to a person's anointing or area of expertise that I open my people and myself to the unknown.

I don't want someone getting up and preaching just anything. Neither do I want someone practicing foolishness on my members. Since I am fully accountable to God for the sheep, whatever comes out of the mouth of someone whom I invited to minister becomes my responsibility, whether it is good or bad. If the person preaches heresy, then I am liable for it. If he preaches New Age doctrines, I should not be upset when the people begin to act on what they heard.

When getting someone to minister at my ministry, I first want to know where his area of strength is, as I've previously stated. I also would prefer that the person came by way of recommendation from another minister, particularly one who I am in covenant with. Usually when one minister recommends another, the guest minister feels a sense of accountability to the one who referred him. He is less likely to do or say something stupid knowing that he can be reported to another trusted fellow minister.

Finally, you should get to know the minister over a period of time. There are various ways to get acquainted with people. It could be something as simple as having a series of conversations with the person on the phone to try and get an idea of what his spirit is like. You might want to go out to eat with him. Jesus used that method to get closer to His own disciples. If you want to know how the person ministers, ask him to send you a teaching tape.

Ask the prospective guest minister to send you the best tape that he has in his collection. Listen to the tapes. If you have time, you may want to go and listen to the minister preach in person at another place where he might be ministering. It may take a little time to build relationships or to make striking discoveries. Do whatever it takes to get to know the person. The bottom line is that the people whom you allow to minister before the sheep should not be total strangers to you. Often those who are strangers to you are also strangers to God.

My brethren, be not many masters, knowing that we shall receive the greater condemnation (James 3:1 KJV).

29. | *Confess God's Word daily.*

O ne of the main secrets to success in life and in ministry is meditating on and confessing God's Word daily. In Jewish synagogues you can often hear people reciting the Torah each Sabbath day. It is this recitation and meditation of the books of the law that is the secret of many Jewish people's prosperity. Since the Word of God is not limited to Jewish people only but is also available to "whoever believes," confession of God's Word will produce prosperous results in your life as well.

I have personally adopted this method as my daily routine. As a result, I have come to discover that confessing God's Word has ushered whole life prosperity into my life. After you make it a practice to confess God's Word on a regular basis, in time you will become a believer of what you confess. You actually start believing what you say even though you may not have the physical evidence yet. One of the special things that happens with words is that the words you confess literally get into your spirit and your subconscious mind. When that happens, you begin to act out those things that you believe.

As you begin to act out those things, you start receiving manifestation, or tangible results. Confession really does bring possession. If you continue to confess that you are healed in Jesus' name, it will bring about healing within your mind and body. With your tongue you actually have the power to create the atmosphere that you desire. God's Word is the ultimate authority on all matters in heaven and on earth. So when you confess His Word, you are speaking His perfect will into existence. His Word becomes your living reality.

Locked within the Holy Scriptures are all the secrets to perfect health, perpetual wealth, and spiritual wholeness. It would be a wonderful thing if all believers knew that. Many people who are not born again understand the power of God's Word and use it to their benefit, especially in the area of financial and personal achievement. Often people within secular society will borrow verses from the Holy Bible and use them for their benefit. They'll make up a phrase like "positive confession" or having PMA, which is an acronym for "Positive Mental Attitude." They'll package it and label it and sell it all over the world and make millions.

The only thing that they are doing that many Christians do not do is make confessions of God's Word regularly. When they do it, they may do it in a disguised manner, but they are still sending out the same message. For example, success coaches and sales experts may say during their presentation or seminar, "I'm on top, and I'll never be down again." They'll get everybody at the workshop or seminar all psyched up repeating this confession until it becomes their own.

The attendees might believe that the workshop facilitator has discovered a new theory when in reality he hasn't discovered anything new at all. Deuteronomy 28:13 says, *"And the LORD will make you the head and not the tail; you shall be above only, and not be beneath, if you heed the commandments of the LORD your God, which I command you today, and are careful to observe them."* They are simply confessing the same idea that is consistent with the Scriptures. They are simply paraphrasing the words, and paraphrasing isn't much different from what Bible translators do each day to make the Word of God more comprehensible to you. No wonder people in those circles receive such favorable results.

Another example of the secular using the sacred can be clearly seen in the rise of commercials and advertisements about debt freedom. There are literally dozens of commercials that try to get people who are in debt to join a debt freedom organization or follow a debt-free curriculum on their road to eliminating their debts. The program that they offer for a percentage based fee usually starts with a careful evaluation to determine exactly how you got into debt in the first place.

Right after that's determined, the debt-free coaches will begin to usher their students into a process of confessions about being better stewards over their money, spending less, and investing more. They'll say things like, "I will not bury my treasure in the ground. I will trade my treasure for a greater treasure. I will be a responsible steward over the money that has been entrusted to me." These sayings all sound great. Not only do they sound great, they also sound very familiar, perhaps from God's Word?

Please don't misunderstand me; I'm not trying to claim that these businesses are not worthwhile. For many people these businesses are very worthwhile. And in many cases it is some people's only hope of ever seeing daylight again, financially speaking. What I am trying to get you to understand is that if we just confess what God's Word says, we will get tremendous results without having to spend our money with these firms. The sayings that I mentioned above are directly correlated to the parable of the talents.

> *Then he who had received the one talent came and said, "Lord, I knew you to be a hard man, reaping where you have not sown, and gathering where you have not scattered seed. And I was afraid, and went and hid your talent in the ground. Look, there you have what is yours." But his lord answered and said to him, "You wicked and lazy servant, you knew that I reap where I have not sown, and gather where I have not scattered seed" (Matthew 25:24-26).*

If you read the story of the talents and accept the message that the story is trying to convey, and then make a practice of confessing God's Word, you too will reap the blessings that the two-talent servant and five-talent servant reaped. What you need to say is, "I am a five-talent person and I will always multiply what God puts in my hand." When you do that, you are confessing the Word. Not only that, but you are also setting the stage for your confession to come to pass. Confessions such as these are not merely words to strengthen your emotions or to rev you up.

When you confess God's Word, you are confessing a time-tested, proven strategy for success that is more than two thousand years old. In that time, His Word has had a zero rate of failure. I don't know how I would ever have been as successful as I am as a ministry leader if I did not repeat His Word every day. I am sure that I would have failed by now. Naturally, this powerful tool of confessing that which you meditate on is not limited to the area of finances. It applies to every area of life.

You should make righteous confessions in the areas of your family, relationships, health, institution growth and development, and salvations. As long as you've got God's Word, you'll be fine. Confessing God's Word helps me not to focus on my limitations, my insufficiencies, or my personal failures. I stay clearly focused on God's track record, realizing that His Word has never nor will ever fail.

But his delight is in the law of the LORD, and in His law he meditates day and night (Psalm 1:2).

This Book of the Law shall not depart from your mouth, but you shall meditate in it day and night, that you may observe to do according to all that is written in it. For then you will make your way prosperous, and then you will have good success (Joshua 1:8).

30. Be a model of what is important to you.

━━ ✠ ━━

Whatever is important to you and whatever you desire to see in your people, you must model first as an example. For example, if you as a pastor have declared that "praise and worship is very important to me," then you must become the model of what you expect. If you want to see men, women, and children in your church praising and worshipping God, then you must become the model of what you desire.

You can't be in your office reading your Bible or watching television while the praise and worship service is going on. That sends a mixed message. You should be the very first person in the service praising and worshipping God. In fact, you should be the example that leads everyone else into the presence of the Lord. If you say that it is important to you, you must model it.

If you believe that punctuality is a trait that God wants you to lead in demonstrating, then you cannot be late for service under any circumstances. You have to model what you expect. You need to be at the service before everyone else.

I have heard pastors sharply rebuke their congregation, warning them that God despises slothfulness and that they should judge themselves in the area of punctuality, especially since Jesus is coming again soon. Although the people truly desire to respect their pastor's wishes by being on time, they cannot. They can only replicate the example that they have seen modeled in front of them. This is most people's train of thought: "If my pastor has a late spirit, then I too will feel quite comfortable being late." So if you are late, leader, don't get upset when your members are even later than you are.

There's no difference in the area of giving. If you want your ministry people to give big offerings and to give sacrificially, they will first have to see that level of giving being performed by you. I make it an intentional practice to have my people witness me giving large offerings to the Lord. That way not only do they hear me talk about sowing seeds, they regularly see me doing it.

I am not doing it to be seen or to get the praises of men. I am fully aware of the Bible passages that condemn such arrogance and pride. Those kinds of givers already have their reward.

There is an old adage that says, "People don't do what you tell them to do; they do what you do." This is very true. You can warn a small child not to say curse words, but if they continue to hear their parents use curse words, they'll only be capable of following the same example that their parents set for them. People only do what they see you doing. So make sure that whatever you say you expect from the people, you lead out first in making your desire come to fruition.

But when the chief priests and scribes saw the wonderful things that He did, and the children crying out in the temple

*and saying, "Hosanna to the Son of David!" they were indig-
nant and said to Him, "Do You hear what these are saying?"
And Jesus said to them, "Yes. Have you never read, 'Out of
the mouth of babes and nursing infants You have perfected
praise'?"* (Matthew 21:15-16)

31. | *Never take credit for something that God is doing.*

Keep in mind that although God shares His authority, under no circumstances will He ever share His glory. God shares His authority by distributing authority gifts to men—the apostle, the prophet, the evangelist, the pastor, and the teacher. But for whatever He does, He wants to receive all the glory. Stay humble! You ask, "How can I remain humble?" It is very simple. Give God credit for everything.

You must always be careful to let the people know that you cannot do anything unless God empowers you to do it. Here at our ministry we have built a wonderful edifice to the glory of God. I worked with the builders and was very actively involved in the entire process from start to finish. But when I behold our new sanctuary, the only thing that I can say is, "Look what the Lord has done." It wasn't Grant that pulled this one off. I could have never done it because I have limitations.

However, in God there are no limitations. And as long I wholeheartedly put my trust in Him, He won't allow me to fail. But I have to recognize that it is God doing the work, so I take no glory for it. The Bible speaks of an earthly king, King Nebuchadnezzar, who decided to take credit for God's work.

One day the king stood on top of the roof of his mansion. As he began to look out over the mountain ranges and the plains, he began to believe that everything he saw was not only his, but also a direct result of his might and power.

He began to believe that he built Babylon for his own majesty and not the Lord's. God was quickly disgusted by the king's arrogance and immediately began to set him straight. The first thing that God did was to take away Nebuchadnezzar's authority. There is a very strong message here. God will revoke your authority when you do not give Him the glory. If God is going to trust you with increased authority, you are going to have to give Him increased glory and credit for what He has done and is doing. Let's read this passage:

All this happened to King Nebuchadnezzar. Twelve months later, as the king was walking on the roof of the royal palace of Babylon, he said, "Is not this the great Babylon I have built as the royal residence, by my mighty power and for the glory of my majesty?" The words were still on his lips when a voice came from heaven, "This is what is decreed for you, King Nebuchadnezzar: Your royal authority has been taken from you. You will be driven away from people and will live with the wild animals; you will eat grass like cattle. Seven times will pass by for you until you acknowledge that the Most High is sovereign over the kingdoms of men and gives them to anyone he wishes." Immediately what had been said about Nebuchadnezzar was fulfilled. He was driven away from people and ate grass like cattle. His body was drenched with the dew of heaven until his hair grew like the feathers of an eagle and his nails like the claws of a bird (Daniel 4:28-33 NIV).

King Nebuchadnezzar began to push God's most sensitive button, the one about glory. In other words, God never wants it to be a question about who takes credit for His handiwork. Every time you take credit for what God is doing, you remind him of what Satan did when he tried to hog all the glory to himself. I've seen ministers lose churches because they began to take credit for God's work. That has to be the quickest way to lose all your authority.

If you preach a sermon and a hundred people get saved, it's not you who saved them. You didn't convict them of sin. Jesus saved them, so give Him the glory. If your ministry is experiencing phenomenal growth, God gets the glory, not you. If your budget is more than a million dollars, it's not because you're so wonderful. It is because God has favor on your ministry. Everything that you have is a direct result of His faithfulness, not yours. Never take the chance of getting on the wrong side of God by trying to assume credit for something you know you haven't done. In all things give God the glory!

This was the LORD'S doing; it is marvelous in our eyes (Psalm 118:23).

32.

Whenever the people's countenances change, so will their hearts.

+→ ⊷✦⊷ ←+

tart studying people. Study their facial expressions. Notice how people's faces will change. A person's countenance will tell an entire story. His countenance will reveal things about him that words cannot. I have never been shy about communicating with people. I have never talked a whole lot, but I am a pretty intent listener. Therefore I notice far more about a person than if I talked constantly. People who talk all the time aren't able to recognize what's actually going on because their garrulousness becomes so overwhelming.

If a person does not want to be actively involved in the ministry, I can tell by looking at his face. I can tell how a person responds to an offering raised in my honor by simply looking at his facial expression. It is quite interesting that you can actually judge whether a person is wholeheartedly committed by his countenance. When a person's countenance begins to change, it is a clear indication that his heart has changed also.

Don't allow people's countenances to change without interceding for them. Some problems can be averted; others cannot. I would like to avoid all the ones that can be avoided. Most people become known by their dispositions. Some people are sweet people by nature. Some folks are very talkative, and others are extremely quiet. Some people are hyperactive; some are calm and peaceful. When you have determined what kind of countenance a person regularly has, and he becomes the total opposite of what he is known for, you've got a situation on your hands.

When people get ready to leave your ministry, or when they've decided to backslide against God, their countenance will change. When that happens, it can be somewhat intimidating for a leader. But don't wait; pray for them and address what needs to be addressed.

> *So the LORD said to Cain, "Why are you angry? And why has your countenance fallen?"* (Genesis 4:6-7)

33. Don't give loans or make financial investments with members.

—✦—❈✦❈—✦—

L ending money to friends is one of the main ways to destroy your relationship with them. It's no different when it comes to your members. One thing I have noticed is that most ministry members automatically believe that the minister always has money simply because of the position he holds. They believe that he never experiences financial challenges. That is not necessarily true. And in most cases it's not that way. There are wealthy ministers and then there are far more broke ministers than you would ever realize.

Even the ones who are broke are often looked upon as rich in the eyes of the people they lead. Because of that, people are often inclined to ask the minister to lend them money when they get in a financial bind. Lending them money is a horrible mistake. First, they are probably in their financial bind because they failed to manage their money properly in the first place. And if they can't manage their money, what makes you believe that they will pay you back? You are not a bank.

Lending money is why the bank exists. Feeding the sheep is why you exist. Let your people know which banks and loan institutions are willing to loan them money. If they cannot borrow money from a conventional loan institution because their credit is horrible, then they need to repair their credit first. Not in all cases, but in many, people who borrow money hastily are usually high-credit risk.

If the bank streamlines whom they lend money to, you should too. The Bible suggests that you should never lend what you are not willing to lose. If you can't afford to take a thousand or ten thousand-dollar hit, then don't lend it. I have always found it to be more beneficial to sow a seed into someone's life rather than give the person money. If I sow a seed, I am setting myself up for a return, and God always blesses seed-sowers.

You may ask, "What if a person needs to borrow money to go into business? Is it all right to lend him money then?" Perhaps you may want to go into business with that person as a joint venture. Again you need to be very careful and extremely prayerful when entering business ventures with your members. I understand that as a leader you may not be paid as well as you need to be. You may desire to earn some additional money to help subsidize your income. In this case, you need to know all the facts up front.

You also should be very cautious not to go into business with or lend money to just anybody. You should know who the person is that you wish to be partners with. Personally, I suggest that you choose to do something without too much involvement from your people. They really need to see you as their leader. Most members cannot handle seeing their minister in other capacities and tend to become too familiar with them. Trust God instead; He will supply your financial needs.

My son, if you become surety for your friend, if you have shaken hands in pledge for a stranger, you are snared by the words of your mouth; you are taken by the words of your mouth (Proverbs 6:1-2).

34. Be patient; your labor will produce fruit if you are fulfilling your call.

⸻ ⊰⧓⊱ ⸻

If you are truly called to do a work for the Lord, don't expect your beginning to always be glamorous. In fact, your beginnings may make others question whether you were actually called. So don't focus on where you are right now. If God called you to perform a work, then fruit will come in due season. Focus more on how you expect to finish than on how you start.

Back in the late 1980s, the Los Angeles Lakers were a winning basketball team. In fact, they won the national basketball championship in 1987. However, if you were to watch any of those old games on videotape, you would immediately discover something about the Lakers. They did not look very pretty during the first half. Often they lagged behind the competing team by as much as twenty points. That did not matter to them, though. They did not care about how they looked during the first half. They knew that they were going to win. And that they did.

During the second half you would think that they were anointed by the Holy Ghost to play basketball. They came out looking like a totally different team. When they won the game, they did so by ten to twenty points. It looked liked they were going to lose in the beginning, but in the end they increased abundantly.

You may be small now, but that's all right. You are not at your end. If you make it your business to stay focused and to keep moving forward taking progressive steps, you will become stronger with each step. After a while, you will be amazed at how much progress you have made. If you are doing what God told you to do, just keep on doing it. Be consistent! Don't try to do what another ministry is doing; that will only distract you from your assignment.

As with most leaders, you may sometimes wonder when God will do what He promised to do in your ministry. You may often think, "I've been doing this for so many years now, and I still do not see the type of fruit that I believe I should be experiencing at this stage of my ministry." The very nature of fruit is that it must go through several seasons, not just one year, before it can be consumed into the body. If you plant an apple tree this year, you will not be able to eat the apples in the same year that you planted it. Even if apples do come in the next year, they'll taste horribly sour and be as hard as a brick.

Why? They are not ready yet. They have to go through a seasoning process before they are ripened. Your ministry is the same way. Just because you are small does not mean that you have to be ineffective. You can be small and powerful. Consider Gideon's army. God reduced his army from 32,000 soldiers to a measly 300 men. That reduction was a part of Gideon's process. God orchestrated the events in that manner so that He would be able to get all the glory after the battle was fought and the victory was won.

Your ministry will have great victories also. God did not call you just for nothing. He called you to make a difference. However, everything has a season and a time. When your season arrives, not only will it have been worth the wait, but you also will have a much more profound respect for the lessons that you learned along your journey. Be encouraged, for in the second half you will shine. You will win!

Though your beginning was small, yet your latter end would increase abundantly (Job 8:7).

35. | *Live within your means.*

⊶ ⊱⊰ ⊷

S top trying to get things you cannot afford. Perhaps you have heard people or maybe even ministers tell you that you need to stretch. That may be true in certain circumstances, but not all. You need to stretch when your faith is bringing you to the higher level where God desires you to be. You don't need to drive a Mercedes Benz 600SL if you earn only $30,000 a year. That's not operating by faith. That's being foolish.

God increases you when you live within your manifested means. I rarely if ever see God bless a person who intentionally creates debt situations that he cannot manage to pay for. If God did not order it, then He is not obligated to pay for it. God is management minded. Because of that, in virtually every situation He is trying to get you to learn the lessons and the laws of good management. Learning how to manage your household expenses and not creating more in the process is a great training ground to qualify yourself for managing far weightier matters such as God's kingdom work.

If you purchase things that you cannot afford in your own personal life, then it is highly likely that you will purchase things that your ministry can neither afford nor does it need. If you have fifty members, you don't need to purchase a thousand chairs. If your budget is only $100,000 a year, you can't afford an Allen Pipe Organ. Some models can cost more than $220,000 after installation. That's more than twice your annual budget.

Your day is coming. There's really no need to rush it. For now, drive what you are able to pay for. Live where you can pay your mortgage without killing yourself. If God so desires to increase you, then let Him enlarge your territory. When He does it, all the costs involved with your territory expansion will have been paid in full.

On the other hand, when you force the issue, you wind up having to pay for the bill when it comes due. Manage your way to more. If God places you in a seventy-five-seat room, make sure that your room is the highest quality meeting place of its kind. Do your best with what God has already given you. When you do that, you will begin His process of qualifying you to receive more.

> *For which of you, intending to build a tower, does not sit down first and count the cost, whether he has enough to finish it—lest, after he has laid the foundation, and is not able to finish, all who see it begin to mock him, saying, "This man began to build and was not able to finish"* (Luke 14:28-30).

36. | *Make it a practice to have regular sex with your spouse.*

This may seem an odd principle to include in this book, but it really is important. Sexuality is one of the most beautiful expressions of love that God has given for a man and his wife to share. God uses sexuality as a means of encouragement between two married lovers and to provide the infrastructure for which we can produce creative ideas that will ultimately benefit the kingdom of God. My warning to both men and women in the ministry and those who are laypeople is this: *Do not give place to the devil.* Don't allow your spouse to be out in a position where he or she will long for another person simply because you have refused to have sexual relations with him or her.

I have always been a bit bothered by the widely known fact that more unmarried people have enjoyable sex than married people. I realize that this is the plan of the enemy. In fact, many married couples appear to have such a boring marital life that single people would rather stay single because they don't believe marriage is worthwhile and exciting. As a Christian believer, your example of marriage should be one of sheer excitement.

By your example, you should make single people want to get married when they see how much fun you and your spouse are having with each other. Singles should never be able to look at your relationship and say, " If that is as good as marriage gets, then I don't want to ever get married." If single folks give that kind of commentary on your marriage, then you may need to rethink and revamp your entire marriage, especially the image that you are giving off to people.

Some of the older ministers used to say, "Sex ain't important. It's not everything." It's true that sex is not everything. It is not that all-and-all in marriage, but it is very important. It is at the point when you begin to act nonchalantly about sex that the devil comes in your marriage and tries to destroy it. Of course, lack of sex is just one of the many roads that the enemy may want to use to cause marital destruction. Don't let him use it. Be there for your spouse and his or her personal pleasure—and that pleasure should always be a mutually enjoyable adventure.

If you are not having sex regularly with your spouse, the enemy has already set in place many willing candidates who will oblige. Sex should not be something that you do only on special occasions, holidays, birthdays, and anniversaries. It should become a customary practice in your marriage. In the same way that you should never become too busy to pray, you should not become too busy to have sex with your spouse.

Prayer produces a much-needed intimacy with our heavenly Father. Without prayer our spirits begin to rapidly decline and become weakened from spiritual abstinence. Sexual intercourse produces a much-needed intimacy with your spouse. Without it the flesh begins to search out alternate methods of satisfaction. Usually those alternate methods do not bring glory to God. If you've gotten too busy to make love to your spouse, then you are far too busy, and in time something's going to give. Don't let it be your marriage!

Let the husband render to his wife the affection due her, and likewise also the wife to her husband. The wife does not have authority over her own body, but the husband does. And likewise the husband does not have authority over his own body, but the wife does. Do not deprive one another except with consent for a time, that you may give yourselves to fasting and prayer; and come together again so that Satan does not tempt you because of your lack of self-control (1 Corinthians 7:3-5).

37. Nothing will happen until you make it happen.

G et started! If you don't do something, nothing will ever happen. There will be times when, if you are going to do something for the Lord, you will not have the time to wait on another person's vote. In addition to that, you can't wait for people to get things started for you. You must take the initiative.

Things don't simply happen; there must be an intentional effort on your part. Until you begin a fund designated for building your new edifice, you will never raise any money. Unless you initiate a collective soul winning effort to win the lost, people will continue to perish for the lack of knowledge. The reason you've not purchased the land you need is because you haven't located it yet. And the reason that you have not located it yet is simply because you have not searched for land.

In life things just don't come to you. God's blessings tend to come to people who are already actively in the process of doing something. The old folks used to say, "When you make one step, God will make two." What message were they trying to get across? They were trying to let us know that nothing of lasting value will ever happen for us until we first do something.

The ten lepers in Luke 17 desperately wanted to receive a healing touch from the Lord. In order for them to receive their healing, though, they had to first do something. First they appealed to Jesus Christ to have mercy on them. Then they showed themselves to the priest. Their healing came as they went, or in other words, as they did something. You would be surprised at how much God will do in and through your life once you take the first step.

Whatever the thing is that you have been believing for or that you have been wanting to do for so long, just do it. Remove all your customary excuses. Take away your spirit of doubt and disbelief. It doesn't matter how many people are part of your ministry or how small your budget is. If God has placed something within your heart to do, just do it. Take those first baby steps toward your goal. For example, if God told you to purchase some property yet you don't have enough money for the down payment, God still expects for you to do something that will display your faith in God.

If you haven't any money, it could be something as simple as making an appointment with the realtor to actually see the property. At least you are doing something. Perhaps you can visit Home Depot or Lowe's hardware store to begin picking out the various decorations for the inside of your building once you've purchased it. That's doing something. You can get on your knees in prayer and ask God to help you to formulate a plan of action to acquire the property. Again, you are showing initiative.

If these lepers had done absolutely nothing, they would have received absolutely nothing in return. They would have continued to be ostracized by the people within their society. They would have never been able to enjoy the freedoms that people who are healed and whole enjoy. It could very possibly be that you are holding up your own blessings and supply simply because you refuse to do anything. God will work wonders once you've decided that you will no longer allow lethargy to stand in the way of your supply. Go for it!

> *Now it happened as He went to Jerusalem that He passed through the midst of Samaria and Galilee. Then as He entered a certain village, there met Him ten men who were lepers, who stood afar off. And they lifted up their voices and said, "Jesus, Master, have mercy on us!" So when He saw them, He said to them, "Go, show yourselves to the priests." And so it was that as they went, they were cleansed* (Luke 17:11-14).

38. | *Always speak well of your spouse in front of other people.*

The way that you treat your spouse will set the pattern for how your ministry members will treat him or her as well. Some leaders have a very poor self-image and are unusually insecure. They don't like to publicly promote their spouses because they believe that it takes away from them. They wrongly think that their people won't look up to them as highly if they have to share the spotlight with their spouses. Little do they know that when you promote others, you are promoting yourself in the process. Humility attracts greatness. Humility promotes you.

One thing that always turns me off is when a man disrespects his wife publicly or privately. God refers to a wife in the Scriptures as a *"good thing"* (Proverbs 18:22). Someone who is good should be treated as such. In the same manner, wives should honor their husbands. I am always very careful to acknowledge my wife. I know far better than anyone else how invaluable she is not only to my children and me, but also to the success of our ministry.

Without her, there would be a serious void. She plays an extremely important role in the life of our ministry. Because of that, I make it my business as the head of my ministry to let the people know that I affirm her. In times past, particularly male ministers would keep their wives in the background. She was often treated as window dressing. Her purpose was to sit on the front row and just look pretty. Her role was limited to being the overseer of the women's department or in charge of the kitchen ministry. Well, those days are over now.

God is using women in various capacities in His kingdom. And they are doing a wonderful job in those roles. Whether you agree or not, you and your spouse are one. That is how God designed marriage to be. Because of that you should always speak well of your mate. If you talk down to him or her, not only are you setting a terrible precedent for the members to follow, but you also are demeaning yourself in the process.

It is our job as ambassadors of the Lord Jesus Christ to build up each other in the body. We are commissioned by the Lord to strengthen the brethren. If God has called you to be a person who strengthens and encourages others, there is no better person to start with than your own spouse. Don't keep it a secret; publicly let everyone know how much you love your spouse. Your positive words will create an environment that will cultivate healthy growth in your ministry.

John bore witness of Him and cried out, saying, "This was He of whom I said, 'He who comes after me is preferred before me, for He was before me' " (John 1:15).

39. | *Always be willing to be mentored by your mentors.*

※◆※

No matter how long you study under a great teacher, remember that the student is never greater than the teacher. You may eventually lead a larger ministry, have a more successful business, oversee a larger budget, or even have a greater worldwide television ministry. But no matter how much you grow and increase, you are still the student. The student is always learning and gathering wisdom from the teacher. In fact, as the teacher gets older, even more knowledge can be gathered from him.

Even when the teacher passes on to glory, your mentoring process is still not over. At that point you are still perfecting what the master has taught you over the years. You will always be able to recollect gems that you have gleaned over the years. There are things that I have been taught by my previous leaders that I now can use today. I wasn't able to implement those things before because it was not the right timing.

The success of my ministry can largely be attributed to my being mentored by great men of God. You can have all the book knowledge in the world, but if you don't know how to submit yourself to the teaching of a master, you will inevitably fail in life. Talent comes and goes. One of the great challenges that many ministries deal with in our modern day is lack of men within the church.

One of the root causes for this lack can be directly correlated with man's inability to be taught. Most men have natural proclivities to become great leaders. However, far too few of them are willing to be taught by someone who has proven to be successful in the area that they need instruction. I have heard men say things like, "I'm a man like he is. What can he tell me about anything? He isn't any better than me." When men speak such vain words as these, little do they realize that they are killing their only possibility of becoming successful in life.

There is no way to become successful unless you are taught how to become so. Self-help books are still one of the best-selling categories in the publishing world. Why? People are tired of making the same mistakes over and over again, so they've decided to get some help from the experts. You can chance trying to be your own plumber and make an entire mess of your home, or you can buy a book on how to be your own plumber. That is good. But the best way to become a plumber is to become an apprentice and be personally mentored by a master plumber.

There were twelve disciples, each of them handpicked by Jesus. All the disciples witnessed the miracles that Jesus performed. They saw Him bring dead people back to life, cast out demons, cause blinded eyes to suddenly see, and turn five loaves of bread and two fish into a catered feast for five thousand people. Although they saw Him do such wonderful miracles, few of the disciples could perform the miracles that Christ did.

One of the saddest passages in the Bible is found in the Gospel of Matthew. It deals with a man who had an epileptic son. This man sincerely desired for his son to be healed of this sickness. He did what any ordinary thinking person would have done. He brought his son to Jesus' disciples. Wouldn't you expect Jesus' disciples to be able to help this child? After all, they walked with the Lord in the most literal sense.

> *And when they had come to the multitude, a man came to Him, kneeling down to Him and saying, "Lord, have mercy on my son, for he is an epileptic and suffers severely; for he often falls into the fire and often into the water. So I brought him to Your disciples, but they could not cure him"* (Matthew 17:14-16).

The disciples could not cure him because they did not fully receive the mentoring that Jesus offered. Interestingly, there were twelve disciples, yet over half of them are not mentioned very much in the Scriptures regarding their lives. Half of them did not do anything much. Some people can follow you to the ends of the world yet never get your spirit and character. You have to desire to be mentored. You have to want to be like the person who is teaching you.

One reason our jails are so filled up with strong and healthy men is because most men are not teachable. Having an unteachable spirit will always produce trouble. Brothers and sisters in Christ cannot be jealous of people who are living better than they are. Instead, learn from them. If a leader has a more excellent ministry than I do, I am not be jealous at all. I use that as an opportunity to learn as much as I can from him or her. I don't have a problem being mentored. Neither do I have a problem with mentoring a person who really is serious about being trained.

Ministers and other spiritual leaders must be willing to invest more time into young men and women to teach them the basics on how to win in life. Many of our young people don't even know the basics of how to live. In every area of life we are witnessing failures at an all-time high. People are failing in the ministry, failing in politics, failing as governmental heads, and failing as educators.

When does this mad cycle of unnecessary failure end? We will begin to see winners emerging from the ashes only when teachers once again begin teaching and students begin learning the lesson. Our public inner-city school systems are living proof of what I am saying. Some teachers are so frustrated, having gone to college for six to seven years to earn a degree in teaching, yet having no one interested in learning.

At the same time, our children are going to school feeling as if their main concern is to protect themselves from the criminals within the educational system. It's all madness. Mentoring is the cure. But you have to be willing to be taught. And then you must be willing to give back that which you were taught. In order for us to make any sizable progress, we have to first become humble. We have to start desiring to be like someone in this earth realm who has a Christ-like character. Model that person, learn from him or her, and win.

A disciple is not above his teacher, nor a servant above his master. It is enough for a disciple that he be like his teacher, and a servant like his master. If they have called the master of the house Beelzebub, how much more will they call those of his household! (Matthew 10:24-25)

40. | *Maintain covenant relationships.*

A covenant is a binding agreement between two parties that cannot be broken because it was created in love. For example, a husband and wife do not merely make vows one to another; they make a covenant. True covenants cannot be severed. There are people who I am in spiritual covenant with for the rest of my life. In the event that I am ever in a troubled situation, I know that I can depend on my covenant brothers to be there for me.

But more than that, each person who I am in covenant with brings a certain dynamic to our relationship that enriches our union. There are some people who are gifted in certain areas of life and ministry more than others. As a covenant brother I am obligated to give whatever I am gifted with to my brother or sister in Christ. Everybody has a role to play.

Suppose you are building a new house in a subdivision near your city. Each person brings an element that is needed in order to complete the house. For the house to successfully be completed and for the town inspector to issue a certificate of occupancy, you will need a number of gifted individuals doing their parts to build a quality house. You will need a framing carpenter, an excavator, a plumber, an HVAC person, a roofer, a finish carpenter, a painter, a drywall contractor, a person to lay tile, a carpet layer, an electrician, and a landscaper. And even that list is not complete.

The point is that every person on the list brings a needed characteristic to the house. Without it the house will lack. What would a house be like if it were almost fully complete yet did not have running water or workable toilets? How about if your home was complete except for one thing—there was no heating system installed and you lived in Alaska? Hopefully you are getting my point. We need each other not only to survive but also to be refined and become better.

That is why I don't really search out friendships. I am not really interested in just being anyone's friend, nor am I interested in finding someone to just hang out with. I'm far too occupied for that. What I am always in the market for is God-sanctioned, God-organized relationships with brothers and sisters who can help me in areas that I lack and to whom I in turn can contribute my strengths.

When God connects two people in a covenantal sense, it's far greater than just another person to call a friend or associate. God is actually sending help. More often than that He is sending you an answer to your prayers. I meet a lot of people when I travel around the country to speak or when I attend conferences. Often people I meet will ask me, "Doc, when are you going to let me come and speak at your church?" That approach can turn me off sometimes.

The reason that can turn me off is because when people come off with that kind of attitude, it sends me a message that they are not interested in covenant. And if you are not interested in being in covenant, you can't really help me or my ministry members. People who are in covenant with you are not always trying to get something from you (money, notoriety, fame, position, or even a preaching engagement). They are more interested in trying to give you what they have.

People with that kind of heart are the kind of people I want to have around me all the time. They aren't just hanging around me for the fish and the loaves. Rather, they want to be in my presence because they sincerely love me. The beginning of growth in your ministry, friendship, or marriage happens when you begin to understand how important true covenant is.

I am in covenant with Jesus Christ not for what He can give me, but for what I can give Him. When you are truly connected you'll never have to worry about whether or not the person with whom you are in covenant will reciprocate the favor. You do your part and he will naturally be inclined to do his. God has already finished His part, and now is your turn.

But Naomi said, "Turn back, my daughters; why will you go with me? Are there still sons in my womb, that they may be your husbands? Turn back, my daughters, go—for I am too old to have a husband. If I should say I have hope, if I should have a husband tonight and should also bear sons, would you wait for them till they were grown? Would you restrain yourselves from having husbands? No, my daughters; for it grieves me very much for your sakes that the hand of the LORD has gone out against me!" Then they lifted up their voices and wept again; and Orpah kissed her mother-in-law, but Ruth clung to her. And she said, "Look, your sister-in-law has gone back to her people and to her gods; return after your sister-in-law." But Ruth said: "Entreat me not to leave you, or to turn back from following after you; for wherever you go, I will go; and wherever you lodge, I will lodge; your people shall be my people, and your God, my God. Where you die, I will die, and there will I be buried. The LORD do so to me, and more also, if anything but death parts you and me." When she saw that she was determined to go with her, she stopped speaking to her (Ruth 1:11-18).

41. | Stop fishing for cleaned fish— they do not belong to you.

B efore a person actually gets born again, in most cases he has been prayed for and ministered to by more people than you can imagine. More than that, the Holy Spirit has been working with that person for quite some time to bring him to the point of repentance and conversion. When that person becomes a part of the body of Christ, then he is ready to duplicate himself, making disciples in others.

Some leaders spend a lot of time trying to get people who are already saved to join their ministry. That is not only senseless, it is fruitless. The whole purpose in evangelizing the world is to grow the kingdom of God. God's kingdom does not grow exponentially when one disgruntled person chooses to leave his old church and join mine. That's not the objective of the kingdom of God. Our objective should be centered on getting the lost delivered from their impending destruction.

All of us as believers should collectively pursue methods to reach the masses with the message of Christ's saving power. There are some ministers who get overly excited when churched folks start coming to their ministries. What you should do is get sad when churched folks come. More often than not, they left their former church over a contentious situation. So when they join your ministry, you merely inherit a problem and all the drama that goes with it.

There are so many souls in your community who need to hear your message that it really should be a crime for you to focus your attention on fish that are already swimming in someone else's tank. Think about it this way: For every person who is already churched whom you are trying to woo away, you could have possibly reached ten unsaved people. Regroup, and rethink exactly why you were called to minister God's love in the first place.

And He Himself gave some to be apostles, some prophets, some evangelists, and some pastors and teachers, for the equipping of the saints for the work of ministry, for the edifying of the body of Christ, till we all come to the unity of the faith and of the knowledge of the Son of God, to a perfect man, to the measure of the stature of the fullness of Christ; that we should no longer be children, tossed to and fro and carried about with every wind of doctrine, by the trickery of men, in the cunning craftiness of deceitful plotting, but, speaking the truth in love, may grow up in all things into Him who is the head—Christ—from whom the whole body, joined and knit together by what every joint supplies, according to the effective working by which every part does its share, causes growth of the body for the edifying of itself in love (Ephesians 4:11-16).

42. Never make critical decisions when you are tired.

W hen you are tired, you cannot think logically. As a result, you will make foolish decisions. Some people are so disoriented when they are tired that they appear to be drunk. I believe that over-tiredness is one of the tools the enemy will use on believers to cause them to enter into foolish agreements and situations. If you truly love the Lord, for the most part you are not going to get involved with an outlandish kind of sin, and the enemy knows that.

So if he cannot get you to commit a foolish act, he'll convince you to omit a needed thing—sleep. Perhaps I need to remind you again that you work for the King of kings. It is your responsibility to be on hundred percent alert at all times when you are on duty. The enemy always tries to catch you off guard. He tries to catch you sleeping when you should be guarding.

If you are ever in a situation where you have to make a critical decision yet you are bum tired, ask the other person if he can wait until later. Buy some time. You have too much to lose from making a hasty, thoughtless decision. In the heat of the moment people have made stupid decisions that have cost them large sums of money, their marriage, their family, and worse yet, their entire future. Think things through with a sober and rested mind. If you do that, I'll guarantee you that your effectiveness will more than double.

> *But he himself went a day's journey into the wilderness, and came and sat down under a broom tree. And he prayed that he might die, and said, "It is enough! Now, LORD, take my life, for I am no better than my fathers!" Then as he lay and slept under a broom tree, suddenly an angel touched him, and said to him, "Arise and eat." Then he looked, and there by his head was a cake baked on coals, and a jar of water. So he ate and drank, and lay down again. And the angel of the LORD came back the second time, and touched him, and said, "Arise and eat, because the journey is too great for you." So he arose, and ate and drank; and he went in the strength of that food forty days and forty nights as far as Horeb, the mountain of God (1 Kings 19:4-8).*

43. | Never use God's money too freely without consulting Him first.

＋ ≣✦≣ ＋

God owns everything. Everything belongs to Him. Even the money in your pocket really belongs to the Lord. As good stewards we are obligated to ask God if we have permission to use His money. We cannot freely spend His money on just anything. Some people are unusually wasteful, and wastefulness is a sin.

I realize that different people have different views on what wastefulness is. Some folks falsely believe that driving an expensive automobile or living in a palatial home is wasteful. That's not being wasteful. That is being extravagant, and we serve an extravagant God. There is nothing wrong with having the best that life has to offer. In fact, God wants us to have the best things that life has to offer. However, He does not want us to be wasteful with His money or resources.

When I got saved as a teenager, I remember the elders preaching about the story of the prodigal son. As I grew up in age and in the things of God, it began to dawn on me that their emphasis was placed more so on the boy coming back home. They would preach messages about the prodigal son every time a backslider came to visit the church. They'd get real emotional when they got to the punch line, "Come back home, you sinner. Come home. Jesus is waiting with open arms. Come home."

People did get saved, and that was wonderful. However, there was a totally disregarded message in this story. That message is this: Don't be wasteful. In other words, you should never spend or invest your money where you are not going to receive a return. God is the kind of God who wants us to put our money not in safe places but rather in productive places. The word *prodigal* literally means wasteful. This wasteful son of a rich man spent his money on worthless things. After he had spent all his money, he had nothing.

I want you to realize that the money God has entrusted you with has great potential. It can build great structures. It can feed hungry people and shelter homeless persons. It can clothe the naked and help educate the illiterate. The right amount of money can produce phenomenal results. But it is when you choose to waste God's money that He becomes angry. The consequence is that your supply will be limited from then on.

If you really want to know exactly how God wants you to deal with His money, just ask Him. God has so much work that needs to be financed in this earth. He is counting on you to help Him get the job done. The one-dollar bill or hundred-dollar bill that is in your pocket—whichever applies—does not belong to you. It belongs to the Lord. Anything that could have been used for a better purpose becomes a waste.

Always ask yourself, "Could I have used this money for something better?" If you could have, then you should have. You may ask, "How will I really know whether I am being wasteful or extravagant?" It's simple. If you spend your money on something that you do not use, then it's a waste. Don't purchase clothes, cars, houses, or even food and not use it.

It's not a cute thing to have dozens of clothes in your closet that you don't wear, especially since there are thousands of people who would appreciate wearing them. If you don't use it, it becomes a waste. Your car is not made to sit in your garage. It's made to be driven. Don't build a church if you are not a worshipper. That will only be a waste. Let us think before we act with God's money and commit to be wiser stewards with it than we have ever been before. As with anything else, God will hold us responsible for our actions.

For every beast of the forest is Mine, and the cattle on a thousand hills. I know all the birds of the mountains, and the wild beasts of the field are Mine (Psalm 50:10-11).

The earth is the LORD'S, and all its fullness, the world and those who dwell therein. For He has founded it upon the seas, and established it upon the waters (Psalm 24:1-2).

44. Concerning societal issues, determine that whatever God hates, you will hate also.

⊷ ≑✦≑ ⊶

The Bible says we are ambassadors of Jesus Christ. What does it mean to be an ambassador? That means you represent the King in all matters. So when it comes to controversial matters in society, you stand with your government, the KOG (Kingdom of God). An ambassador speaks only on behalf of his government. An ambassador never has his own opinions on a matter. His opinion really does not matter.

For example, if someone were to ask you, "How do you feel about gay marriages?" As an ambassador of the kingdom of God, you cannot legally answer that question. You must reply, "Sir, I cannot answer your question as posed. I can only answer based on my constitution, which is the Word of God. And my constitution declares homosexuality and lesbianism to be an abomination to the Lord. My constitution declares that all sinners will have their part in the burning lake of fire and brimstone."

When you represent the King, you don't have a say, or even a voice. Your voice becomes His voice on all matters of spirituality and righteousness. That brings me to my next point. Since you are a loyalist to the King, anything that hinders the progress of His kingdom is something you must be against. So whatever God hates, you must hate. Whatever God loves, you must love.

There is no compromise in this area. If you are going to be a representative of Christ, you have to take a stand. You've got to take sides. You must not forget that biblical Christianity is not like what we see today. The early Christians were constantly persecuted because of the stand that they took against unrighteousness and because of their faithful commitment to follow the teachings of Jesus.

I wholeheartedly believe that if you are going to be a biblical Christian that you too will come up against great fire and persecution, especially when it comes to matters of controversy. I am always a little uncertain about people who call themselves Christians yet who have never been talked about, criticized, or persecuted. The bottom line is that we as believers have already made our decisions on all matters that pertain to godliness from the time we accepted Christ into our lives.

That decision cannot change. The decision that we made to follow Jesus and His Word is what will define us in a wicked and perverse generation. It's what identifies us as Christians. People ought to know that you stand against sin and unrighteousness. It shouldn't be a question on the matter. Just say it now: "I love what God loves, and I hate what He hates."

For the zeal of thine house hath eaten me up; and the reproaches of them that reproached thee are fallen upon me (Psalm 69:9 KJV).

45. Daily pray for those who have rule over you, and teach those under you to pray for you.

⊷ ⩤⬥⩥ ⊶

One thing that I have found to be an indispensable tool is prayer. Prayer has stopped wars. It has saved people from being destroyed. The prayer of faith has healed the sick and raised the dead. Prayer has been the backbone of many great spiritual institutions. In addition to that, prayer is what makes leaders great. I believe that the success of my ministry can be largely contributed to prayer. People in my ministry pray for me. And I appreciate their prayers more than anything in the world.

Prayer compensates for the areas that you are weak in. If you love your leader, you should feel obligated to pray for him not every once in a while, but every single day. Your prayer for your leader is the equivalent to a person receiving a meal each and every day. Would you want to go without eating for weeks at a time? I would surely hope not. In the same manner your leader cannot afford to go without your regular prayers. It is spiritual nourishment for him.

A pastor I know recently had a nervous breakdown. He felt as if he was carrying the entire weight of the ministry on his shoulders. He believed that he was doing everything all by himself and did not have the support of the people. It got so bad that he decided he wanted to just give up and quit. When he called his leadership team to inform them about his feelings, they all sheepishly confessed one by one that they had not been praying for their pastor on a regular basis. Even the pastor's wife admitted that she prayed for her husband only every week or so, not every day.

The leadership team repented and promised that from that day forward they would never allow the enemy to attack their man of God again. You can literally ward off the attack of the enemy when you pray for your leader. If the enemy has already successfully launched his attack against your leader, you can still do something about it. You can pray. Your prayers will lessen the effects of the enemy's attack.

I pray for those whom I am submitted to every day. I know that if they fall, it will have an effect on me and my ministry members. That's far too much to lose. If all I have to do is pray and God does the rest, then I shouldn't have anything to complain about. You pray; God will do the work; and your leader will have God's protection and favor. When that happens, God's favor will come on your life as well.

> *Praying always with all prayer and supplication in the Spirit, being watchful to this end with all perseverance and supplication for all the saints—and for me, that utterance may be given to me, that I may open my mouth boldly to make known the mystery of the gospel, for which I am an ambassador in chains; that in it I may speak boldly, as I ought to speak (Ephesians 6:18-20).*

46. | Use repetition as a teaching tool.

W hen you teach, be repetitious. It has been said that repetition is the mother of skill. There is no better way to get people established in the truth of God's Word than to get them to hear the same Word of God over and over again. When people hear a message for the first time, they are inclined to forget most of what they heard as early as two hours after hearing it. If they hear the message repeated over a five- to eight-week period, it will remind them of what they have heard. After a while they will no longer need to be reminded because they will know it.

Marketing professionals understand the power of repetition well. Companies spend millions of dollars to develop witty slogans that will be remembered for generations. Just think about the commercial lines you hear on television. I am sure that if I started one, you could finish it. What about Maxwell House coffee? "It's good to the _____." Did you say the "last drop"? How about Burger King—"Have it your way." And Kentucky Fried Chicken—"It's finger lickin' good."

All these slogans are just a reminder of how powerful hearing something over and over actually is. The more you hear it, the higher your chances are of believing what you hear. Can you imagine if you told your children from the time they were small, "You are rich"? I believe those children would become rich long before they reached adulthood. What they hear will become a part of them. If you want things to stick with the people, you have got to keep on saying it.

Your mental rate of retention increases greatly when you hear something over and over. And if I sense that there is a deficiency in a certain area among my members, then I am going to teach on that area for several weeks.

In the early days of our ministry some people seemed to think that preaching in a series was redundant and monotonous. That didn't bother me at all. I knew that God was using my repetitious preaching style to build something of value in the life of each believer. There were people who would say, "Brother Grant, you've been preaching on tithes and offering for the past twelve weeks. I think everybody has gotten the point by now." My first question to this person would be, "Have you begun to bring your tithes and offering to God's house honestly and faithfully?"

More than likely such a person would cower down from his confrontation since he had not been paying his tithes. Very often people will complain about the minister teaching too long on a topic that is convicting them. That is all the more reason to continue to preach God's Word. Some other members erroneously believe that God will tell them to tell the leader what he or she should be teaching. They'll say, "Brother, you need to preach on the rapture and water baptism."

Usually people are not responding to the right spirit when they do this. So the more effective thing for you to do is to continue preaching and teaching the word that God has placed in your heart. You may not see tremendous results in the first week or so. Just keep teaching. In time you'll see an army of trained soldiers ready to defeat the enemy because they have been properly trained in the Word of God.

> *For this reason I will not be negligent to remind you always of these things, though you know and are established in the present truth. Yes, I think it is right, as long as I am in this tent, to stir you up by reminding you* (2 Peter 1:12-13).

47.
Everything that you experience in your ministry will be directly correlated to your faith.

Y ou can't build anything of lasting value without faith. Faith is that component that builds strong institutions. It amuses me when I hear other ministers label me and others who teach like I do as "faith preachers." I really don't know how a person can be a preacher at all and not preach faith. Every minister should be a faith minister.

A man or woman of God simply cannot work for God without faith. Just look at Hebrews 11. All the successful saints used faith. Moses parted the Red Sea and let more than a million people through the desert by faith. Abraham walked across the breadth and width of a land by faith. By faith Gideon defeated a mighty army with only a handful of men. Even God created the worlds with faith! If God uses faith, shouldn't we?

Your ministry will grow in correlation with your faith. Faith is not an option; it is a command. *"The just shall live by faith"* (Romans 1:17). We all have a measure of faith, but it is up to us to use it. It is part of the very fabric of our life in Christ.

Now faith is the substance of things hoped for, the evidence of things not seen (Hebrews 11:1).

But what does it say? "The word is near you, in your mouth and in your heart" (that is, the word of faith which we preach) (Romans 10:8).

48. | *Don't be afraid to make plans.*

╌ ═◈═ ╌

I f you fail to plan, then you might as well make plans to fail.
Everything that we do in our ministry is planned. We didn't
just decide one day to start our building project and then
the following day begin to build. No, first we made plans with
the architect on how we wanted the building to be designed.
Then we scheduled regular meetings to discuss all the details.
We planned whom we were going to use to construct each
phase of the project. The day that we expected to start con-
struction was planned long before we started. Because of all
our planning, we now enjoy worshipping in a state-of-the-art,
first-class sanctuary.

We don't arbitrarily choose people to minister at our
church. Long before a guest speaker comes, I know that he has
been invited to come. I know why he is coming. I know what he
is an expert at. We leave nothing to chance.

Even the messages that I preach each Sunday are planned at
least a month before I preach them.

I realize that there are some people who, especially as it
relates to services, will say, "Brother Grant, we don't plan

anything in our service. Planning is another way of asking the Holy Ghost to leave. In our ministry we welcome the Holy Spirit. And we don't make plans that will interrupt His flow." Although that sounds real spiritual, it's not the way that God expects us to do things. We have plans that are clear and written, and God anoints them for His glory.

Don't be afraid to make long-term and short-term plans. Without a destination, the journey is merely a meaningless waste of time.

Any enterprise is built by wise planning, becomes strong through common sense, and profits wonderfully by keeping abreast of the facts (Proverbs 24:3-4 TLB).

Then the LORD answered me and said: "Write the vision and make it plain on tablets, that he may run who reads it. For the vision is yet for an appointed time; but at the end it will speak, and it will not lie. Though it tarries, wait for it; because it will surely come, it will not tarry (Habakkuk 2:2-3).

49. | *Favor is greater than and usually precedes financial wealth.*

I f I had to choose between money and the favor that God gives, I'd choose God's favor every time. There is nothing in life that equals the favor of the Lord. When you have God's favor on your life, He will cause you to have favor with people also. And when you have favor, it is worth far more than money. Favor gives you access to areas that money cannot even buy.

I recommend that you study the life of Joseph. His life is a perfect example of a person who found favor in the sight of the Lord and his fellow man. The Bible says in Genesis 39:4, *"Joseph found favor in his eyes and became his attendant. Potiphar put him in charge of his household, and he entrusted to his care everything he owned"* (NIV). Throughout his life, Joseph really never needed large amounts of money because God gave him favor.

Everywhere he showed up, he continuously rose to the top level of management and governorship. In Potiphar's house the favor of the Lord allowed Potiphar to trust Joseph to manage and properly care for all his earthly possessions, including his licentious wife. Then when in jail unjustly, God's favor caused Joseph, when in jail unjustly, to be above all his fellow prisoners. Eventually God brought Joseph into a level of high influence in Pharaoh's court. Pharaoh appointed him the governor of the state.

No matter where Joseph was, he automatically ascended to the top. He did not exalt himself as so many leaders try to do today. God exalted him because of favor. Your ministry will be a hundred percent less burdensome to you once you realize that you can't do everything by yourself. There are some jobs that will be accomplished only when God's favor comes. So seek His presence, seek the face of the Lord, and shortly after you'll receive His favor.

And I will give this people favor in the sight of the Egyptians; and it shall be, when you go, that you shall not go empty-handed (Exodus 3:21).

50. | *God has already given you enough to get started with.*

E verything that you will ever need to succeed in ministry and in life, God has already given you. All you have to do is use what you have been given. When you use what God has already given you, you set yourself up to receive more from the Lord. This is a spiritual law. I have heard so many ministers complain about what they do not have. They'll say, "If I had about three hundred members, I could really do great ministry in my town. I could take the city." Or they'll say, "If I had a million-dollar budget like your church, I could impact my city for God too." The list of "ifs" goes on and on. "If I had an organist…if only I had a good choir director, youth minister, children's pastor, administrator, assistant pastor, foreign missions director…then I would do things, too!"

The thing is, you really don't need any of those things in order to be successful. Having people fill positions is a good thing, yes. But just because they fill certain positions does not necessarily mean that your ministry could not function well without them. The people who you already have, whether they are ten or ten thousand, have been sent to you by God to help you fulfill the vision of God on your life. You must begin to view each person as a God-given gift in order to receive the full benefits that God intended him to be to your ministry.

You can't look at people thinking about how good it would be if you had a better replacement. People can sense your deepest feelings about them. Focus instead on the quality that you have in front of you. "What if the people are not quality people—then what should I do?" If that is the case, God sent them to you to build and enhance. It is your responsibility to bring out the best in them.

One of the things that I have come to learn and understand is that the work of the ministry is one test after another. After you pass one, the next one will follow. If God can trust you to properly manage a budget of hundreds of dollars each week, then He will promote you to manage thousands then tens of thousands of dollars each week. But you have to be faithful with whatever He entrusts you with.

If God has given you ten members, minister to those ten members just as diligently as you would ten thousand. Sow your time into developing those members. You will be surprised at the amazing results you'll receive when you use what God has already given you. Having more should never be your objective. Having more of anything in life is always a direct result of how you use what you already have in your possession.

Begin to practice this law of use. Actually, you have already begun by simply reading this book. You could have chosen to let this book sit on your shelf with all the others that collect dust. But instead you made the quality decision to read and take its contents to heart. That action puts you ahead of so many others who choose to do nothing. You will be amazed how God will continually increase you as you take the little that you have and put it in the Master's hand.

> *Do you not yet understand, or remember the five loaves of the five thousand and how many baskets you took up? Nor the seven loaves of the four thousand and how many large baskets you took up?* (Matthew 16:9-10)

Jesus took five loaves and fed five thousand people. How did He do it? He didn't hire a caterer to feed them. That would have been quite convenient. But no, He was able to multiply the little that was in a young boy's hand and make it increase to get the job done. I promise that He will do the same thing for you as soon as you begin to employ the resources that you already have in your possession. If you have an upright piano, then play it to the glory of God. In time God will give you a grand piano.

If you have a minivan, then fill it up every Sunday with people and bring them to church to hear God's Word. In time God will give you a fifteen-passenger van and maybe even a fifty-seven-seat coach bus. God has an amazing way of taking your little and making it become more. You have the right amount of people, the right amount of money, the right amount of faith. Use it and watch it grow.

> *He who observes the wind will not sow, and he who regards the clouds will not reap* (Ecclesiastes 11:4).

> *Then he who had received the one talent came and said, "Lord, I knew you to be a hard man, reaping where you have not sown, and gathering where you have not scattered seed.*

And I was afraid, and went and hid your talent in the ground. Look, there you have what is yours." But his lord answered and said to him, "You wicked and lazy servant, you knew that I reap where I have not sown, and gather where I have not scattered seed. So you ought to have deposited my money with the bankers, and at my coming I would have received back my own with interest. So take the talent from him, and give it to him who has ten talents. For to everyone who has, more will be given, and he will have abundance; but from him who does not have, even what he has will be taken away" (Matthew 25:24-29).